Life After Suicide:
The Survivor's Grief Experience

By Terence Barrett, Ph.D.

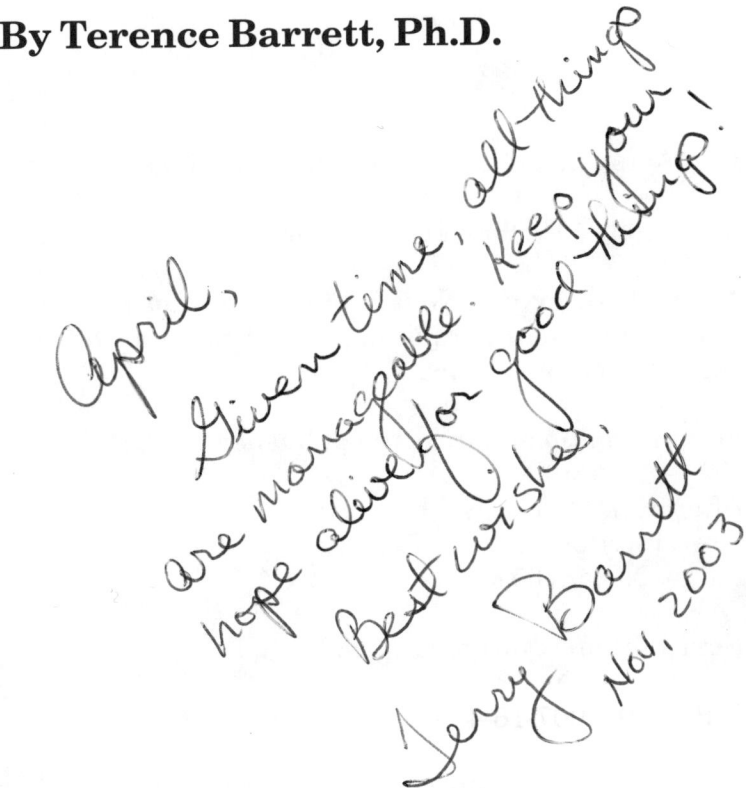

April,

Given time, all things are manageable. Keep your hope alive for good things!

Best wishes,

Terry Barrett

Nov, 2003

Aftermath Research

Life After Suicide: The Survivor's Grief Experience

For information address the publisher:

Aftermath Research
University Station Box 5551
Fargo, ND 58105

First Edition / November, 1989

ISBN 0-9664758-0-1

Designed and Printed by Richtman's Printing, Fargo, ND

TABLE OF CONTENTS

DEDICATION

This book is dedicated to John and Denise, their families, to my friend Tom Hruby, and to the many survivors who warmly welcomed me into their lives and trustingly shared their grief experiences with me.

ACKNOWLEDGEMENTS

I am grateful to God for the grace of inspiration, to Dr. Thomas Scott for his help and support during the initial stages of my research, to Sister Jane Walker and Lana Palmberg for their encouragement and assistance in contacting suicide survivors, and to the many professionals, some of whom are cited in this book, whose efforts have increased our understanding of the survivors' grief experiences and provided direction for my own work.

LIFE AFTER SUICIDE:
THE SURVIVOR'S GRIEF EXPERIENCE

PREFACE

This book provides a description of the experience of survivors after suicidal death; of their struggles to deal with suicide and incorporate it into their own personal life histories, and of their efforts to reconstruct their lives in its aftermath. The material presented here is based on the growing literature on suicide survivorship and on interviews of survivors of suicide, accident, homicide, and natural death bereavements.

The impact of suicide, as in any death, most assuredly varies depending on the type and closeness of the relationship lost. For example, the experience of a wife whose husband completes suicide will differ in many important ways from a father whose son takes his own life. Although the impact of a suicide is greatly determined by the closeness of the relationship which had been formed with the decedent, no one associated with this form of death can escape its effects, regardless of distance from the deceased. Suicide touches something deep in the core of our humanness, and we can, none of us, be neutral to its occurrence.

Among the adult survivors who shared their experiences with me were fathers and mothers, husbands and wives, daughters and sons, sisters and brothers, and "just" friends and lovers. By far, a majority of the survivors had been spouses or parents of the deceased. Not surprisingly, all suicide survivors do not share the same grief experiences. Every survivor experiences death in a unique style, and no one is likely to encounter the entire array of grief reactions presented in the following chapters. On the other hand, most adult suicide survivors, regardless of relationship to the deceased, will identify with much of the experience described here.

My hope in completing Life After Suicide is that it will provide insight into suicide survivorship, not only for those who experience, first hand, another person's self-destructive act, but also for those who interact with the survivors in the aftermath of the death. It would be a blessing for survivors if people they encountered after the experience of a suicide were more understanding and sensitive to their concerns.

CHAPTER ONE
Suicide: A Way of Dying

"Once every minute, or even more often, someone in the United States either kills himself or tries to kill himself with conscious intent. Sixty or seventy times every day these attempts succeed."

Karl A. Menninger [1]

Suicide. Self-inflicted, deliberate, and intentional death. It is one of four ways life officially ends in the United States. The other three ways are by accident, homicide, and by natural cause. Today, in our nation, suicide is considered among the ten leading causes of death. Everywhere, death by suicide outnumbers homicides. It does not discriminate between sex, race, creed, nationality, intelligence, health, social status, success level, occupation, marital status, or age.

Statistics regarding this official form of death are widely and readily available. They are, however, somewhat troublesome. Depending on the information source, suicide can be considered relatively rare or frighteningly common. Some professionals, citing rates like one suicide per every 10,000 people in theUnited States, view suicide as a rare event. Others view this act of self-destruction as endemic within our society, offering numbers varying anywhere between 20,000 to 50,000 suicidal deaths per year. Some experts, like Hirschfeld and Davidson [2] believe as many as ten times the number of people officially reported kill themselves each year. It is estimated that about four percent of our population attempts to complete suicide every year. Estimates of total suicide attempts annually range anywhere from 350,000 into the millions.

Regardless of a person's stance on the prevalence of suicide within our society, it is illuminating to think that the names of individuals who kill themselves would, in one or two years' time, easily fill the Vietnam veterans war memorial, which sadly lists the names of those killed in the entire course of the Vietnam War.

The difficulty with suicide statistics is that they are, by the very nature of the act, incomplete. This difficulty results from two factors, how suicide is defined and how it is reported.

1

Official definitions of suicide usually require that death must occur due to the deliberate intention and self-inflicted completion of a person's wish to die. Yet, in many deaths the intent of the victim to die is not clear and must, therefore, remain undetermined. For example, in some cases, when the decedent intended to end his life, the death might appear accidental, as in a single-car automobile accident. In other cases, the intent on the decedent's part to die might have been absent, although the death appears to be a suicide. This might be true of some gunshot wounds self-inflicted during handling of a weapon and of some homicides that look like suicides. In deaths such as these, the victim's intent to die is not completely, or undeniably, obvious. Regardless of how these deaths are officially listed, they remain "equivocal deaths" in terms of cause.

In addition to equivocal deaths, the true extent of self-inflicted death is concealed by various prejudices surrounding the reporting of suicides. Reporting a suicide is a difficult matter, especially for those closest to the event.

Family members are particularly, and understandably, sensitive about social attitudes toward suicide. Dealing with the implications inherent in a suicide often takes a tremendous emotional toll on the family. Protecting themselves and the memory of the decedent can become a serious concern. It should not be surprising, then, that family members sometimes hide the suicidal nature of the death, if at all possible.

Medical and police officials can be sensitive to the hardships suicide brings to a family. They will often report the death as an accident if the true nature of the death can be concealed. Furthermore, there are religious and bureaucratic complications that arise with a suicidal death. These often make it easier to label a death accidental or equivocal when possible. Finally, differences in coroners' procedures and post mortem examinations regarding the findings of equivocal deaths make the distinction between accident and suicide neither consistently clear nor painlessly reported. Many coroners will list a death as accidental or equivocal, even if the evidence leans more heavily toward suicide.

The numbers of suicides reported in our country are already worthy of our concern. Yet, it is likely that the many prejudices regarding suicide and the equivocal nature of many deaths result in understatement of the number of annual suicides.

Who performs this act called suicide?

The question is often asked, in many ways. Who is most likely to suicide? Is this particular suicide unusual? Can a suicide be predicted? Who is most at risk? Questions like these have been examined by researchers for decades.

As stated above, suicide does not discriminate among sex, race, creed, nationality, intelligence, health, social status, occupation, marital status, or age. It can occur just about anywhere. Sometimes it comes as a surprise, other times not.

Ronald Maris [3] states the greatest number of suicides occurs among physically ill, disabled or retired, and socially isolated older men. Apparently, men are at greater risk than women. Currently, three men perform suicide for every one women, although there is evidence that the number of women taking their own lives is rising today.

Incredible as it may seem, the only age group apparently exempt from suicidal death is children under the age of five, even though suicidal death has been officially reported among children as young as three years. Generally speaking, suicide seems likely among men and women between the ages of thirty-five and sixty.

Among our nation's adolescents, 5000 to 6500 lives are lost annually to suicide, the second most common cause of death within this group. Suicide ranks second only to automobile accidents in killing our youth. Approximately 1000 teenagers attempt suicide each day, and once every ninety minutes another of these young individuals succeeds. Quite alarmingly, the number of suicides that occur among youths between the ages of 15 and 24 has tripled in the last twenty years. Today, the highest rate of completed suicides within the young population is among 18-year-olds about to attend college.

There are more suicide attempts than actual completions. In fact, nonfatal suicide attempts occur between six and eight times more often than completed suicides. Women who attempt suicide, but fail, outnumber men three to one.

That suicide attempts do not always succeed suggests that people who attempt suicide, but fail, and people who succeed in completing suicide may be two different types of individuals. Evidence for this includes the fact that some individuals attempt suicide several times without ever successfully bringing their lives to an end. Ronald Maris estimates that 80% to 90% of those who attempt suicide sometime during their lives ultimately die nonsuicidal deaths. Startlingly, on the other hand, as many as 75% of those who complete suicide, do so successfully on the first attempt.

Many people are alarmed that suicidal deaths currently seem to be on the rise. This increase is often attributed to various factors within our contemporary society. Such cause-and-effect statements require close scrutiny, however, and should be considered with caution. For one thing, instead of an ever-steady incline from prior periods, the number of suicides actually varies from one time to another. Large scale phenomena like war, famine, and the state of the world economy affect suicide rates. Therefore, suicide rates go up and down over a long period of time. Today, suicide rates, while certainly high, are lower than they have been at other times in our culture's history.

Although suicide is certainly somehow related to social factors, it is not necessarily directly caused by them. Most assuredly, *contemporary* social factors are not the root cause of suicide. Self-inflicted death has been a reality since mankind has made written records of its history. The act of suicide can be traced as far back as ancient Greek and Egyptian cultures. It is described in the Bible no fewer than six times, interestingly, without hint of sanction or judgment. Throughout mankind's history, there have been times and there have been societies in which the act of suicide was openly accepted and was perceived without disdain, disgust, or disquiet. In fact, it is likely that there has never been a human culture or a time period in which self-inflicted death did not occur.

In light of such facts, it seems inappropriate to focus primarily on modern social phenomena in the study of suicide's cause. The attention really belongs upon the individuals who complete suicide. It might very well be more realistic to look upon suicide as a characteristic of being human, like sexuality, aging, and ultimate mortality. This is not a new concept. Others, like Sigmund Freud, have wondered if self-destructive drives actively opposing the instinct to survive and prosper might not be deeply buried within the psychological makeup of each individual. Everyone has likely met someone they would describe as "self-destructive." A person who seems to seek early fulfillment of a "death-wish" stands out in

4

any crowd. Yet, these are the more obvious examples. There are other human behaviors which are not such blatant expressions of self-destructiveness.

A soldier's cradling himself around a grenade to save his comrades is understandably sentimentalized as a grand gesture of heroic proportions. That is only one perspective, however. In terms of self-preservation and survival, this act could also be considered an extraordinary breakdown in the instinct to prolong one's life to a natural conclusion. We can look closer than this example for self-destructive behaviors. In fact, no individual acts instinctively in his or her own best behalf at all times.

There are times when we just do not take very good care of ourselves. This might take various forms like not eating nutritiously, having poor sleeping habits, overworking, abusing narcotics, smoking, drinking, or eating too much, driving dangerously, taking risks, and indulging in sexual promiscuity, to name just a few. Can these be considered breakdowns in our human tendency and drive to survive? On an even more personal level, a great many people not outwardly self-destructive have, at one time or another, considered suicide for themselves. Most people have probably, at least, wondered what it would be like to bring about their own death.

It seems safe to say that all individuals have entertained self-destructive thoughts, acts, or behaviors at different times in their lives. This suggests that self-destructive drives, though more apparent in some people than in others, do seem to be an ingrained part of our humanness. If this is a fact, it makes more sense to search for the meaning of suicide within individuals than it does within the social fabric of our contemporary culture.

The Study of Suicide

The reflective and investigative attention of modern scientific research has often been turned toward suicide. In the investigation of suicide, professionals have made great efforts to understand, deter, and prevent suicide. They have undertaken to discover whether or not suicide is a result of a genetic inheritance. They have studied character traits and personalities to see if certain ones might make a person especially prone to suicide.

5

During this investigative search, psychological autopsies have been performed on the lives of those who have completed suicide. Differences between people who actually succeed at suicide and those who merely attempt it have been studied. Speculation about the hidden motives for self-destruction continues to captivate the attention of many researchers. External factors believed by some to lead to suicide have also been studied. Even the many, varied, and imaginative ways people inflict death upon themselves have been investigated.

Without question, research has resulted in a growing understanding of the self-destructive human tendency. However, neither the prevention of suicide nor a reduction in the numbers of people who choose suicide as their way of ending life has been achieved.

This is not to say that professionals working in the field have failed. They have made progress and met with successes. Through their diligent labors, effective methods of dealing with individuals in a suicidal crisis have been developed. Indeed, there are many people alive today who would otherwise have successfully ended their lives were it not for the concerned intervention of others employing such methods. It remains, however, nearly impossible to predict which individual, at which time, and under which circumstances, will complete suicide. The opportunity to activate crisis intervention methods, therefore, does not always occur.

Additionally, the human motivation for self-destruction has not been, and most assuredly cannot be, eliminated from the human psyche. If an individual chooses to end his own life, for whatever reason, there are enough opportunities and enough lethal methods available for him to do so. When a person's own suicidal intent overwhelms him, it seems no amount of intervention, love, or caring will ultimately deter him from a self-destructive course. For this reason alone, preventing suicide within our culture assumes impossible proportions.

This raises a question regarding the utility and effectiveness of suicide prevention and intervention centers located in many communities. While some research demonstrates the influence these centers have exerted in saving individual lives, other studies suggest that suicide prevention services have had little impact upon reducing the frequency of suicides within any given community.

An example is provided by the Samaritan organization. The Samaritans are a group of trained, nonsectarian laymen in the British Isles who volunteer their "friendship" to individuals experiencing a suicidal crisis. The impact the Samaritans have had in communities they serve has been so widely lauded that Samaritan branches have been organized in many other countries, including the U.S. Yet, studies of the Samaritans' overall effectiveness in reducing suicide rates have been disappointing. Again, although the volunteers have proved very effective in thwarting the self-destructive urges of many individuals on a course toward suicide, they have been unable to either prevent or reduce the occurrence of suicide within their communities.

Can We Ever Accept Suicide?

There are theorists and practitioners within the profession of suicide prevention who have developed a special insight regarding suicide. Though they continue to work to save the lives of people entangled in self-destructive careers, they accept the obvious fact that suicide has not been eliminated from the human experience and that it probably will never be "preventable." They do not necessarily consider suicide as an acceptable death, but they do accept that suicides will occur beyond all efforts invested in stopping them. They do not like the fact that suicides happen, but they accept that they do. In this, these individuals appear to have come to terms with the act of suicide.

There is wisdom in accepting that suicides will occur no matter what external circumstances appear to be in any person's life. Proof that social factors cause or prevent suicide is lacking. Although external social factors contribute to a person's choice to complete suicide, such factors are not the sole cause of self-destructive acts. In fact or fantasy, social engineers might structure a society someday in which the supposed factors influencing self- destructive actions are nonexistent, but it is doubtful any scientific endeavor could ever completely eliminate the human drive for self-destruction. Where there are humans, there will likely be suicide.

One premise developed in this book is that the true weight of social factors does not fall upon people who contemplate or complete suicide. Certainly, social influences definitely have no impact upon the decedent once the act has been completed. The real power of contemporary social factors in regard to suicide is upon the people left behind by the suicide. It is upon the experience of survivors that current social perceptions, beliefs, attitudes, and conventions have a significant influence in the aftermath of a suicide.

This chapter, about the act of suicide and those who choose to perform it, is simply an introduction to an experience that affects millions of lives. Among the four recognized ways of dying in our society, suicide is emphatically different from the other forms of death. It is different because in this single method of death, there is a seemingly obvious choice to die. It is different because there is generally a message conveyed to the survivors that implies more than just the decedent's wish to die. It is different because its performance causes discomfort, disgust, and disquiet within the general society. And, finally, it is different because our present social institutions and conventions typically provide no constructive structures to facilitate or ease the survivor's grief.

How the differences inherent to suicidal death impact upon the survivor is the heart of this book. Hopefully, greater insights about the experience of suicide's survivors, will result in more sensitive perceptions of suicide. Surprisingly, perhaps, it is the survivors who will profit from a more enlightened acceptance of suicide's realities.

Enlightenment allows, rather then prevents, more gentle expression of our humanness. Today, social and moral issues are generally in a process of revision. Former taboos and sanctions are being more widely and more closely scrutinized. In this analysis, they are losing some of their power to frighten and to inhibit. Examples of issues with which our maturing society wrestles include the continuing and growing controversies over abortion, euthanasia, capital punishment, and nuclear armament. The dilemma of suicide belongs among these social and moral issues.

Moral, legal, and medical questions involving a person's right to choose method and time of death are currently under debate and discussion in open forums. The September, 1989 decision of a Georgia Superior Court Judge to allow a paralyzed civil engineer to end his own life by removing himself from life-sustaining medical equipment serves as an example of current trends. It seems evident that opinions among religious, professional, and public domains about these concerns are being challenged and are changing.

Although certainly neither encouraged nor condoned, suicide might be accepted in the future as an act that humans perform, just like it was sometimes viewed in the past. It will not be considered a crime, sin, weakness, mental illness, pathology, failure, or comment against the social and human condition. It will not elicit feelings of disgust, disdain, or shame.

If the debate over suicide is ever resolved, suicide might become a preferred way of dying for *some* people, much as it was in other societies in other times. Kearl and Harris [4] believe the emerging attitudes toward death in our country include the consideration of a person's right to control the form and timing of his or her death. Perhaps by having a choice regarding the time and method of one's own death, by freely and openly dealing with the human motivation for self-destruction, and by thus coming face to face with the reality that death awaits us all, we would all be better able to accept our humanness and the responsibilities for life that are as much a part of being human as are the opposing drives for survival and self-destruction.

It is important that we understand the connections between social views and attitudes toward suicide and the trauma which survivors dealing with self-inflicted death encounter. Any change in the way suicide is perceived and accepted will directly influence the grief experiences of these survivors. It is to a discussion of the survivor's bereavement that the remainder of this book is addressed.

CHAPTER TWO
The Grieving Survivor

"It is the survivors who are the real victims of suicide for their lives are damned and devastated forever."

Louis Wekstein [5]

"Survivor" is a common and familiar name. It is a label often assigned to people who are left behind after another dies. Obituaries name survivors. The media, professionals and clergy frequently phrase bereavement in terms of survivorship. For example, "He is survived by his wife, Mary Ellen, and his two daughters, Pamela and Susan," or more simply, "Survivors include his wife and two daughters" are both expressions of the concept of survivorship following a death. The common use of the label "survivor" obscures how well it describes the experience of those in the decedent's life. A survivor does more than continue to live on after the decedent's death. He or she actually *survives* the death. He or she suffers through and *survives* a bereavement.

During the emotional and traumatic experience of grieving, the life of the survivor is, in many ways, at risk. There is the chance he might not survive at all but might become a fatality himself somewhere in the aftermath of the death. Therefore, when the death is sufficiently past and the bereavement is finished, the individual left behind has truly traveled in harm's way and *survived*. Bereavement after death is passage to a new life, sometimes better and sometimes worse. It is a survivorship. It is the description of survivorship following suicide to which this chapter now turns.

Suicide is sometimes perceived as an intensely private and personal act, as if a person's choice to end her own, single life affects only her. Sadly, this is never true. In most cases, suicide is an event that at least involves relatives and friends. Tensions that result in a self-destructive course are, almost invariably, between two people, whether that be husband and wife, parent and child, or boyfriend and girlfriend. Even suicides that appear to be completely isolated do not take place in social or interpersonal vacuums. Someone must discover the suicide's body. Sometimes paramedics, emergency room personnel, or physicians become involved in futile life-saving efforts. Someone must notify officials of the suicidal nature of the death. Officials must file reports. The coroner, mortician, cemetery personnel, and often times the media, become involved. If the media brings attention to the suicide, many people without knowledge, contact, or emotional investment involving the decedent must deal with the suicide.

No one has a neutral reaction to a suicide. It is an act seemingly able to squeeze strong emotions from each of us. When we have news even of a distant, unknown death by suicide, it can shock and trouble us. Suicide is rejection on the highest scale. Perhaps the person who takes her own life turns her back, in the most extreme manner, upon our society. In the aftermath we question the value of the lives we have made for ourselves. And when we question life, anxieties regarding death are awakened. Dealing with another's suicide, then, turns to reflection upon the meaning of our own lives and inevitable deaths.

The reaction to suicide may have roots deeper than we realize. Quite possibly the emotions unearthed by suicide are not even developed in our own lifetimes. It has been suggested that there is buried within each of us a primitive fear or superstition about death that suicide releases from the shadowy caverns of our unconscious. Does suicide breathe life to an ancestral fear that a dead person extracts some vengeance from those who have been left behind?   Whatever the roots of the reaction to it, suicide unquestionably extracts a terrible vengeance upon the survivors. The extent of this vengeance upon those left behind is described in the following chapters.

G. Ginsburg [6] conducted a study in Reno, Nevada that helps grasp how widespread the impact of suicide is in our culture. Of the people he interviewed, 74% knew one or more persons who had either completed suicide, attempted suicide, or probably attempted suicide. Fifty-three percent personally knew at least one person who had completed suicide. Of these, 21% were family members of the decedent, 37% knew the decedent very well, and another 29% knew the decedent at least fairly well.

Skeptics might rightfully doubt statistics gathered from a single study carried out in one location, especially one like Reno which might be accused of attracting a special kind of person. There are other studies, however, which indicate the enormity of suicide's influence. Edwin Shneidman [7], for example, estimates that the number of family members who survive suicide is between 250,000 and 300,000 annually. Over a period of years, this number swells into the millions. The number of people, including family, friends, and associates who are intimately associated with suicide may be as high as 750,000 a year. In the course of a few years, the number of people who must deal with the impact of suicide becomes staggering.

Those with a philosophic outlook seem to accept that the person who dies has left suffering behind. It is the survivor who must deal with the aftermath of death. Whether or not it is true that our entire population is touched on some emotional level by each individual report of suicide, it is evident that millions of people are coping with this self-destructive act on an intimate basis. It is the grieving survivor closest to the suicide who must suffer the trauma of loss. As, Loius Wekstein [5] says, in the matter of suicide it is the survivor who is the true victim.

The Suicide Survivor as Victim

Historically, the survivor was not always victimized by someone else's suicide. In times past and in cultures long expired, suicide was not considered deviant or criminal. In ancient Greek, Roman, and Norse cultures, and in not so ancient oriental cultures, taking one's life was looked upon as a noble act in many instances. In fact, there were circumstances under which suicide might be dictated by social pressures or custom. These cultures permitted a person to find an honorable solution to many dishonorable or intolerable situations through suicide. To perform suicide was to act honorably and to lend pride to the person's name and memory. The act itself did not necessarily conjure up reactions of fear, shame, or blame nor did it inspire legal punishment, degradation, or revenge.

Socrates is not the only famous person to have selected his own death. There are numerous other names recorded in history who chose suicide as the preferred method of death, including King Saul, Demosthenes, Mark Antony, Cleopatra, Brutus and Hannibal.

The social acceptability of suicide was altered drastically and with far-reaching social impact in the sixth century, A.D. The victimization of the survivor can be traced at least back to that century. Largely as a reaction to the widespread quest for martyrdom undertaken by the early Christians, especially the Zealots, St. Augustine spoke out against suicide and the deliberate engineering of one's own death. Afterwards, in 533 A.D., the Church decreed that suicide was the most deadly of all mortal sins. In the words of Alfred Alvarez [8], "an act which during the first flowering of Western civilizations had been tolerated, later admired, and later still sought as the supreme mark of zealotry, became finally the object of intense moral revulsion." At this point in our social history the persecution of the survivor became sanctioned on religious grounds. From this historical moment to the present day, the consequences for suicide have been borne by the survivor, not the decedent.

Damning a soul to hell or refusing consecrated burial has little impact upon the decedent after the self-destructive act has been completed. The survivor, however, experiences both the worry and concern for the soul of the departed and the hardships and stigma of severely altered funeral and burial practices which, from ancient times, have been designed to ease the sting of death for the bereaved.

Victimization of the survivor received legal sanctification later. In Europe, a person who performed suicide was labeled either a criminal or a lunatic. In either case, the state was legally justified in taking the suicide's property for its own. In this fashion, the family survivors were both cheated of any inheritance due them and were stigmatized by the suspicion of genetically transmitted lunacy.

Laws supporting the victimization of the survivors held on until recent generations. For example, the laws in England permitting the confiscation of a suicide's property were not revised until the late nineteenth century.

It is important to understand the influence of the religious and legal sanctions imposed upon suicide. The cost, or penalty, of suicide could not be borne by the person who performed the so called "sin" or "crime." Afterall, the sinner or criminal was no longer at hand, and the long arm of the law can reach only so far. The consequences, or better still, the punishments for the suicide, if they were to be meted out, had to fall upon the heads of those left behind. In times past those punishments included cruel burial practices, the collection of taxes, the leveling of fines, and the confiscation of property. Beyond the obvious losses, the survivor eventually was seen to somehow share the responsibility for an act in which he had no hand. He became guilty and, therefore, punished for an association with the decedent.

In times present, the circumstances are changed only on the surface of the issue. No longer is the survivor taxed, fined, or cheated of property, except perhaps in the matter of insurance policy payments. Today, the survivor pays the penalty for another's suicide in a more subtle, and perhaps more devastating, manner. The punishments for suicide today are largely emotional and psychological.

Many modern researchers believe the impact of suicide far exceeds that of any other form of death. This is especially true for the family of a person who chooses to end her own life. The surviving family finds it exceptionally difficult to understand the suicidal act of one of its members. The emotional consequences of such an event have been known to endure for excessive periods of time. Loius Wekstein believes that the presence of a person dead by suicide lingers on, festering and hounding the lives of the family and others associated with him long after the decedent's departure. The survivors abruptly left behind endure emotions that might never end or be resolved.

After any death, survivors experience what has come to be called a grief process. Using the word "process" implies that grief involves a number of particular actions, or reactions, and that it continues over a period of time. The manner in which the process of grieving progresses has been studied widely, and many grief reactions have been recognized.

On one hand, the suicide grief process has many features in common with other bereavements. On the other, suicide bereavement is different from other bereavements in important ways, for it is also comprised of grief reactions which are rare in nonsuicidal deaths.

The next chapter begins the description of the grief experience as it is encountered by suicide survivors.

CHAPTER THREE
The Grief Complex

"In the apportionment of suffering, the sting of death is always less sharp for the person who dies than it is for the survivor."

Arnold Toynbee [9]

The sting of death comes in a common and consistent form among all humans. It is a process called grieving, or sometimes mourning or bereaving. Though this process has many different components in various cultures, it is an experience that is shared by all people who have suffered through the death of someone intimately known to them. Before going on to a description of grief following suicide, it would be helpful to first discuss some general concepts about grieving.

Our first impressions of grieving are formed by observing others in grief. As children, we might be witness to adults in our lives grieving. We view grief vicariously on television. We hear other people talk of grief. Even as adults, we continue to learn about and be witness to grief. For example, we may know friends who experience the death of a parent or friend. We watch their grief and may intellectually understand it, but emotionally we can little comprehend its full impact.

Observing someone else's grief does not prepare us for the experience of our own grief. It merely provides a lesson in grief behavior. We may learn how people *act* when they are grieving, but very few of us are sensitive enough to know what a person is feeling when she grieves. Until it is experienced first hand, grief is something that can only be imagined. And because so much of grieving is solitary, private, internal, and unobservable, what we view of another's grief is not preparation enough for the personal experience of it. Therefore, a person who has never experienced the death of someone close is likely to be terribly surprised, if not frighteningly overwhelmed, by the intimate encounter with grief.

Grieving is a natural, human process that occurs with the experience of significant loss, especially that of a loved person. In a description of grief, Edwin Shneidman [10] suggests that the bereaved survivor is likely to be affected as if she were suffering from a disease of known course. "The recently bereaved person is typically bereft and disorganized. Longstanding habit patterns of intimate interpersonal responses are irreversibly severed. There is a concomitant gale of strong feelings, usually including abandonment and despair, sometimes touching upon guilt and anger, and almost always involving a sense of crushing emptiness and loss. There may be serious physical and psychological [features] in the way of heightened morbidity and even greater risk of death."

The experience of grief can be viewed as a combination of two different and somewhat opposing processes. The first process is often referred to as separation or detachment from the deceased. The second is commonly called reconstruction or recovery. While each of these processes is believed to serve a specific purpose for the bereaved, in combination, the dual processes of separation and reconstruction, make up what is commonly called the "grief process."

Separation

Generally, the purpose of the grief process is to enable a person to first separate from the lost loved one and then to reconstruct a life that no longer includes that important person.

The process of separation from the deceased is indicated by the emotional expression of pain, of suffering, of loss. This process embodies the traditional concept of grief and becomes active immediately upon having knowledge of the death. This is the process around which most funeral rites are structured. Through its expression, both the survivor and society acknowledge that death has brought a terrible loss to those left behind.

During the course of separation, others accept that the grieving survivor will not be herself for a period of time. It is also expected that her actions and reactions will be different from before the death. In fact, some behaviors considered out-of-the-ordinary in normal daily interactions are actually expected during grieving. Examples include crying, wailing, incessant talking or oppressive silence, irrationality, obsession with death, breaking or throwing objects, wandering aimlessness or blunted inactivity, and hyperalertness.

The underlying function of this initial process is gradual separation from the deceased. Even when the death can be consciously acknowledged, or evidently known in a person's awareness, the survivor will unconsciously try to hold on to, or bring back the lost loved one. Initially, then, the function of grief is to help the survivor detach emotionally from the deceased. If detachment does not occur, the survivor will cling both emotionally and psychologically to the deceased. In this case, the grief process becomes short-circuited. Additionally, if this first purpose of grief is not achieved, it will take longer for the second grief process to get underway. It becomes less likely, then, that recovery, if it gets started, will be successfully completed either.

Recovery

Reconstruction or recovery is the second process active within grieving. It is the process which brings the survivor back toward a meaningful and satisfying life.

The specific purpose of the reconstruction process is to redirect the survivor's emotional investment away from the decedent and toward new relationships. This part of grieving aides the survivor in building a new life in which the decedent is no longer a present and significant feature. The outcome, then, can be a life that the survivor finds rewarding and full, and in which she can express love and trust freely.

Recovery obviously begins later in the grief process than separation, but the two are active together at some point. Recovery is marked by the gradual diminishing of the strong reactions that immediately follow death. As separation progresses, the survivor slowly learns to pace the process. A balance is gradually reached between grieving the loss of the loved one and participating in everyday life. Moments of severe grief become shorterlasting and less frequent in occurrence. As Colin Parkes & Robert Weiss [11] describe, recovery from bereavement is typically marked by the absence of grief reactions, by the establishment, maintenance, and involvement in helpful and gratifying relationships, and by the achievement of a new quality of satisfaction in life.

Ultimately, with time and efficient grieving, grief becomes a dull ache, a brief memory that now and then intrudes upon an otherwise adjusted life. Parkes and Weiss conclude that good recovery outcomes are characterized not only by adequate functioning in social roles and freedom from physical and emotional symptoms traceable to the grief, but also by emotional investment in the present life, by hope regarding the future, and by a return to a genuine capacity for experiencing gratification.

The Course Grieving Takes

As a process, grieving has an identifiable beginning, an expected course, a conceivable ending, and a purposeful, desirable outcome. Both time and energy are required of the survivor if the process is to be successful. Although both of these ingredients are available to the bereaved, neither of them may be taken for granted. If the survivor tries to shortcut, abbreviate, avoid, or delay the grieving process, emotional and psychological malfunctions or derailings are likely. Grieving takes time and it must be rendered its due.

A survivor can not expect grieving to simply occur and then to be gone, like a wave washing over her on a beach. The survivor does not just stand in the way of grief and allow it to wash over her in its course. The grief process is functional only if the survivor provides concentrated effort which, then, supplies the energy to keep this natural process on a healthy course.

The processes of separation and recovery require a great expenditure of effort to accomplish completely. The survivor must work at grieving if the process is to succeed. The effort supplied to grieving is usually called the "grief work." This term implies that the survivor must *do* something in order to grieve.

Ideally, effective grief work would be powered by knowledge of the physical, emotional, psychological, and behavioral reactions to grief and how best to resolve them. In one sense, the need for such knowledge might seem superfluous. Afterall, grieving is so natural that it might be instinctual. However, the work required to accomplish grieving is not necessarily so natural.

The fact is, *how* we grieve is greatly determined by social and cultural directives, standards, and traditions. Unfortunately for the survivor, socially accepted methods for grieving are not necessarily the most effective ways of dealing with the inner turmoil that occurs. Therefore, though grieving effectively is a skill that could be learned, it is typically acquired only through on-the-job experience.

As in all things human, there is great variety in the expression of grief. This makes it difficult to speak in generalities about the course and duration of the grief process. There are, however, trends and consistencies that occur frequently enough to describe grief as an entity with possible limits.

The Stages of Grief

The literature on death and bereavement provides many fine descriptions of the process, course, and patterns of grief. Included among the most often read treatments of the grief process are those of Erich Lindemann [12], John Bowlby [13], and Colin Parkes [14]. These authors describe the grief process as an observable sequence of events that can be divided into stages. In other words, there are particular things that happen during grieving and, in many instances, they occur within predictable time periods. Consequently, most authors divide the grief process into three or four distinct stages.

Typically, the stages of the grief process are given names like Immediate or Shock Phase, Intermediate or Disorganization Phase, and Final or Recovery Phase. These various stages are suggested to be common among most survivors during grieving and specific grief work is accomplished during each phase. However, a caution should always be added to viewing grief within the framework of stages. Stages are a convenient way for understanding the grief experience. They do not provide an exact description of grief's course. In reality, grieving is an ongoing process, not a series of stages marked by specific events, milestones, or timetables.

Grief stages do not realistically progress from one to the next in order. There is overlap in the activity of the stages. While the work of one stage is predominant, a little bit of the work of another might also be underway. Also, at a point when the survivor is primarily invested in the grief work of any particular stage, regressions and progressions from that stage to another are likely. For example, it is not unusual for a survivor involved in the work of the later recovery stage to experience brief, temporary waves of the extreme sorrow first encountered in the initial grief period.

How long the grief process lasts is somewhat determined by unknown and unwritten conventions in our culture. Our society allots a certain period of time in which the survivor is expected to accomplish the grief work. We might call this the "official grieving period." During this period, the behaviors and activities of grief are expected and condoned. This is the time when society says to the survivor, "Go ahead. We know your behavior is unusual and disturbing, but we will tolerate it because you are in grief." However, when grief behavior goes beyond the accepted cultural limits, it is usually perceived to be abnormal, unhealthy, deviant, or frightening. In many cases, if grief exceeds what is considered normal, the survivor will gradually be abandoned and isolated.

The individuals surrounding the grieved survivor are usually responsible for initiating the closure of the official grieving period. They somehow signal the survivor that there has been enough of grieving. Sometimes this signal is conveyed in a gentle, subtle manner. For example, most comforters patiently listen to the survivor's grief immediately after the death. With time, the willingness to listen to sorrowful lamenting may no longer be extended to the survivor. People uncomfortably change the subject when the survivor tries to talk about the decedent. Also, fewer opportunities to call upon the survivor are taken as time passes. A friend might arrange activities to get her out socially.

Often times, the accepted period of grief is ended by more obvious means than just described. Some survivors are openly berated by those close to them; harshly prodded to be done with their grief. Perhaps scolded that they have cried and carried on enough, they are told it is time to get on with their lives. Remarks like "snap out of it" or "stop feeling sorry for yourself" or "if only you wouldn't dwell on it" are not unusual. They immediately signal survivors that people around them have had enough of their grief.

The process of grieving does not end when the comforters become uncomfortable with it and indicate that it might be time for it to cease. By whatever means the signal to end the official mourning period is passed, from the survivor's perspective it usually comes too soon. The survivor typically would like more time to accomplish the overt grief work; more time to hold on to the deceased and the shared part of their lives. Grief usually goes on far longer than those around the survivor are willing or able to accept or tolerate. If the survivor is to ensure that she is not abandoned by those she needs nor further alienated from the comfort she desires, she must take the grief activity underground.

A survivor learns to put up a front, or at least to try to appear as if everything is alright. Efforts at this point are directed at making sure others feel comfortable around her. Gradually, her interactions, demeanor, conversations, and behavior are brought in line with what others would like to see. Meanwhile, as she deliberately tries to "tough it out alone" or "put it in the past," in the underground recesses of the survivor's mind, body, and soul, the pain continues. The suffering goes on. The sense of loss is not overcome. Grief becomes something internal to which the survivor must somehow respond and in some way resolve. In most cases, from this point on, the work of grief is carried out alone.

A survivor learns to grieve away from others. This is a dangerous development. Grief is like a scab forming over an open wound on its way to becoming a scar. If it is too soon repressed or too deeply buried beneath the gauze and wrappings of socially acceptable interactions and behavior, it can become a festering, easily opened wound. Such a wound has the potential to torment the survivor for the rest of her life. If the wounds of survivorship are to be healed, and the survivor to become fully healthy, grief must be opened to the air.

That others signal the end of the official grieving period is not always the disservice to the survivor it might appear to be. It can be a benefit to the survivor if it does not occur prematurely or insensitively. Without external signals the survivor might wallow indefinitely in grief. This may in fact be what happens to unfortunate survivors who are isolated from social contact for some reason. Enmired in grief, they have no signal or push to remove themselves from it. At some point the survivor can sink so deeply into grief that she is incapable of getting herself out without help. Comforters can, therefore be instrumental in providing the initial impetus for both the separation and the reconstruction processes of grief. They are, however, only the catalysts. The real grief work must always be accomplished by the survivor.

Grief Reactions

The work of grief is to successfully manage and resolve the many reactions that arise after the experience of death. These reactions can be viewed as the elements, or components, of the grief process. Grief reactions are the things that survivors experience in the processing of their grief.

Many reactions to loss are readily observable to people around the survivor. Other grief reactions are basically internal states. These are less obvious and more hidden from view, especially once the official grieving period has been closed.

Reactions to death are not the same in the experience of all survivors. While some reactions might be universal grief experiences, others are rarely encountered. Whether or not a reaction is activated and what its intensity will be is determined partly by the characteristics of the survivor and partly by the circumstances surrounding the death.

The components of grief experienced by survivors in our culture have been very well documented and are described in other fine works. This book describes the grief reactions as they are experienced by a special group of survivors. In the following chapters, the reactions of those who have been subjected to the experience of someone else's suicidal action will be explained.

CHAPTER FOUR
The Tidal Wave After Suicide

"There are essentially only two kinds of mourning and grief and reconstitutive patterns: those which accrue by accident, disaster, homicide, and natural causes and those which relate to the stigmatizing death of a loved one by suicide."

Edwin Shneidman [15]

It is often suggested that the grief reactions of survivors who were intimately associated with a person who performed suicide, are qualitatively and quantitatively different from those resulting from other forms of death. For example, Edwin Shneidman [16] states that, "the survivor of a suicidal death must recover psychologically on a different level from that of people who have suffered a more natural bereavement. Natural, accidental, or even homicidal deaths elicit deep feelings of loss, emptiness, sorrow, loneliness, disbelief, torment, yearning, anguish, and heartache; in the case of suicidal death, these emotions are intensified and aggravated, sometimes to unbearable proportions, by the grim additions of shame, guilt, self-blame, and hostility."

Even individuals who have experienced other bereavements in their lives show evidence that they are not prepared for the trauma and upheaval that accompanies a suicidal death. Shneidman suggests that suicide results in a grief far more intense than any other form of death.

Saying there are two patterns of grieving, those experienced by suicide survivors and those experienced by all other survivors, implies that suicide bereavement is unique. Is it? Are the grief reactions experienced by suicide survivors unknown, unrecognizable, or incomprehensible to other survivors? Is suicide bereavement really different from other forms of grieving? It is important to consider such questions if we are to understand the grief experienced as a result of someone else's suicide.

It certainly seems intuitively and logically clear that, because suicide is a different sort of death, suicide survivorship would be different in form and expression. However, before considering any further whether or not suicide bereavement is truly unique, it will be helpful to explain some of the aspects which make it likely to be different.

Suicide Is Unexpected

First of all, suicidal death is usually sudden and unexpected. In its swiftness, the survivor has typically not prepared for it. Preparation for, or anticipation of, a death may be one of the most important determinants of the survivor's ability to accept the death of an intimate and of the adequacy of the recovery from it. Some researchers conclude that lack of preparation results in unexpected death being more difficult to grieve than death that has been anticipated. Parkes and Weiss [11], for example, suggest that unexpected death, regardless of its cause, occasions the most severe bereavement reactions.

Certainly, suicide is a form of unexpected death. However, that the suicide survivor typically does not have the opportunity to anticipate or prepare for the death, neither completely explains the differences in suicide bereavement nor the impact of suicidal death. Even in instances in which the deceased was ill and death was expected, if death occurs because the ill person performs suicide, the survivor may experience a far more intense grief than would have been occasioned by the natural death.

A Prejudice Against Suicide

A second factor that contributes to the different nature of suicide bereavement is the fact that suicide seems to agitate deep emotional reactions even in people distantly removed from the decedent. It is likely that every individual in our society has deeply developed feelings, biases, or prejudices, against self-inflicted death. Therefore, the reactions of others to suicide are seldom neutral. More than any other manner of death, suicide is likely to generate an almost instinctual reaction of repugnance, judgement, incrimination, blame, discomfort, confusion, hatred, anger, or denial.

The expression of the biases against suicide are just as likely among family members of the decedent as they are among strangers. When a suicide occurs within an intimate relationship, the survivor must come face-to-face with his own biases. How the survivor deals with his prejudices and feelings regarding suicide will greatly influence the course of his bereavement.

The result of biases against self-inflicted death is that death has been categorized into types. In our society, for example, there is normal death and there is suicide. Normal death is comprised of all forms of death which are not suicidal. In this context, even homicide is viewed as normal. Although death is a normal, inevitable feature of being human, suicidal death is believed to be outside the range of normalcy. Since suicide is not normal, it is considered abnormal. As Wayne Weiten [17] states, "Our culture views suicide as an abnormal act to be prevented whenever possible, while some cultures consider suicide to be an acceptable and even courageous act under certain circumstances."

The separation of death into normal and abnormal seems to be based on the intentions of the decedent. The common thread connecting all normal deaths is that the decedent had no apparent intention to die. Suicide is abnormal because the decedent apparently decided to die, intended to die, and engineered the death.

This categorization of death into normal and abnormal is based on arbitrary cultural attitudes. This point will be developed further in the last chapters of this book. It is important here only to suggest that the division of types of death into normal and abnormal results in certain consequences for the suicide survivor. It makes suicide bereavement different.

There Seems So Little To Say After A Suicide

A third factor making suicide bereavement different from other grief experiences derives from the cultural biases against suicide.

When a person experiences the death of someone close to him, our society provides an outlet for grief by extending normal and established patterns of support to him. These social supports include funeral services, religious rites and ceremonies, comforting help and support, encouragement, condolences, well-wishes, acknowledgement of the death, and acceptance of the survivor's grief reactions.

Most of us take these patterns of support for granted because they seem to occur automatically and naturally within the community. When we experience a death, we believe that there will be a supportive social response that is initiated without effort on the survivor's part. Again, we believe in and expect such social response. It is automatic.

Survivors of a suicide are more likely than others to discover that these social responses to death are not so automatic. In fact, these so-called "automatic" social responses may even be denied to them. Although our society has an established ritual structure permitting acceptance for every other type of death, it does *not* for a suicidal death.

The funeral services and religious rites following a suicide are often obviously different. Comforting support for the survivor is often lacking or inadequate. Appropriate condolences seem nonexistent. The death is often denied or unacknowledged by others, so drastically in some instances, that it is as if the decedent had never existed. Finally, the survivor's reactions to the death are less fully understood and less easily accepted.

Is Suicide Bereavement Unique?

Its unexpected nature, the biases against it, and the lack of supportive traditions following it have frequently lead researchers to claim that suicide survivors suffer a grief process that is very different from "normal" grieving. Some researchers maintain that suicide survivorship is actually unique in its pattern, expression, and resolution.

It is unlikely, however, that suicide bereavement is truly unique in a general sense. Suggesting that there is suicide bereavement and then there is all other bereavements may lead to inaccurate perceptions of the suicide grief process. The misunderstandings about suicide itself already adversely impact upon the survivors. More misconceptions regarding the grief they experience can ultimately only add to the survivor's confusion.

Suicide bereavement is not a singular and unique response to a self-inflicted death. By far, it is more similar to other forms of bereavement than it is different or unique.

As John Hewett [18] portrays, suicide bereavement is an accumulation of distinct types of reactions. These reactions, for the most part, resemble those experienced in other forms of grief. Specifically, suicide bereavement is comprised primarily of at least four different types of grief reactions. These are; 1) *common, or "normal", grief reactions* which are present in most experiences of grief, 2) *unexpected death reactions* which result from the lack of preparation for death, regardless of its cause, 3) *other-than-natural death reactions* which are experienced when a death results from other than natural causes, and 4) *suicidal death reactions* which are more likely to be experienced in the event of self-inflicted death than in any other form of survivorship.

The next four chapters describe the various types of reactions frequently reported within the experience of suicide survivors. It is not likely that the individual reactions included within these descriptions are complete nor exhaustive in detailing suicide bereavement. Certainly, survivors may experience other reactions that are not outlined in the following descriptions. However, the grief reactions included in the following chapters are those which appear to be most frequent among suicide's survivors.

CHAPTER FIVE
It's The Same, But Different

"A person's death is not only an ending; it is also a beginning for the survivors."

Edwin Shneidman [7]

Suicide, regardless of the social perceptions of its nature, is primarily a grief experience similar to that suffered by all other survivors. It is the loss of a significant person from the life of the survivor. This means grief following suicide will primarily be comprised of grief reactions common to all forms of grief, whether the cause of death was natural, accident, homicide, or suicide.

This chapter describes common, or normal, grief reactions as they are most frequently reported by suicide survivors. For ease of presentation, these common, general reactions will be divided into initial, primary, and later grief reactions.

Initial Grief Reactions

The initial reactions of survivors experiencing the death of a loved one mark the beginning of the grieving process. In the experience of suicide, the initial reactions of the survivors are, with little exception, the same reactions experienced after other types of death. The description of these initial reactions, including shock, disbelief, and severe sorrow, open this chapter.

SHOCK

The most consistent of the initial emotional reactions experienced by survivors upon learning of a suicide are primarily shock reactions. These reactions, sometimes described as psychic numbing, are similar to the shock experiences of trauma victims. Shock reactions are most evident among survivors unfortunate enough to discover the body of the decedent.

One indication of shock is feeling cold, or an inability to feel warmth. Although this may be a generalized, vague sensation, the feeling of cold may be especially apparent in the hands and feet. A sensation of being or feeling numb is also common.

A survivor in the initial phase of grief often appears to be in a dazed and preoccupied condition. She may perform tasks and go through motions with little awareness of her actions and afterwards may have poor memory of events.

The survivor commonly experiences a state of confusion initially. She may become easily disoriented as to the date, day, and time. She may also find it difficult to recognize where she is at or remember a task she has set out to do. Ironically, during this mentally foggy period there can also be crystallization of certain events or feelings. These the survivor will vividly recall long after the bereavement. For example, the survivor might not be able to forget the expression on a friend's face, the scent of someone's perfume, or a remark overheard in passing. Though the survivor might not recall greeting some people who offered condolences, she may remain painfully and acutely aware that others did not extend their sympathies.

The experience of shock usually includes a general feeling of emptiness, generally described by survivors as a feeling of emptiness in the stomach. Although their nerves are actually open, raw, and terribly vulnerable, many survivors initially sense an absence of feeling.

In other forms of death, shock reactions usually last only a few days, dissipating into other normal grief reactions. However, in suicide the shock reaction may be extended, lasting in part as long as weeks after the funeral. This may be especially true for survivors who have discovered the body of the deceased.

DISBELIEF

Among all survivors, there is a strong tendency to resist accepting the reality that death has occurred. Such denial of death is expressed in many ways.

Denial, or disbelief, is evident in many of the remarks of the survivor. Examples include exclamations of "No!," "This isn't happening," or "It can't be true." The survivor might argue emotionally with the person who brings news of the death. Demands to see the body as proof of the death are also common. Some survivors deny death so strongly that, when viewing or identifying the decedent's body, they will insist it is not the decedent.

Disbelief takes other, more subtle forms. For example, a survivor might continue to daily anticipate the decedent's return home. She might cling stubbornly to habits and routines they had shared or look for the deceased in places they had been together. The survivor might also imagine or make up evidence to convince herself that the deceased is still alive.

Although disbelief is a common experience in all deaths, it takes an odd twist in suicide. Survivors of suicidal death tend also to deny the cause of death, i.e., they deny that death occurred due to a suicidal method. Discounting both the cause of death and the fact that death occurred at all is an additional burden normally not experienced by other survivors. Since denial of the cause of death is almost absolutely unique to suicide, it will be discussed in greater detail in Chapter Eight.

In other forms of death, shreds of disbelief typically endure for periods of several days or weeks. Seldom are the realities of the death avoided as the months right after the death go by. In the event of suicide, however, disbelief, or denial, tends to last longer. Denial is most prominent in the first few weeks following the suicide but has also been evident in some cases as long as months or years after the death.

SEVERE SORROW

The reactions of shock and disbelief gradually give way to intense feelings of sadness. These feelings of severe sorrow are not to be confused with depression. This sorrow is comprised of the grief reactions most widely expected of the survivor and most easily accepted by others.

Survivors experience severe sorrow in many obvious ways. They encounter sensations of physical distress which occur periodically and in waves lasting from minutes up to an hour at a time. They commonly cry, weep, or wail for extended periods. Some survivors frequently feel an obvious need to sigh deeply. Some also experience sensations like tightness of the throat, difficulty in catching one's breath, shortness of breath, and an emptiness of the abdomen.

A general physical lethargy often overtakes the survivor. Physical activity of any degree can become difficult. Short walks, climbing stairs, carrying objects, exercising, even eating can become impossible endeavors. Disturbed sleep, loss of appetite, muscular pains, and general irritability may also be experienced.

It is not unusual for the survivor to try to suppress the intense feelings of sorrow. Most individuals are frightened both by the strength of these feelings and by the sensation of emotions run amuck. However, intense feelings of sorrow can be repressed for only short periods. Eventually, they well up and break through to the surface. When they do, their renewed intensity can be both devastating and overwhelming.

The reaction of severe sorrow is often accompanied by other significant changes in the observable behavior of the bereaved survivor. Intense sorrow can generate increased and troubling anxiety within the survivor. To combat such anxiety, a survivor might turn to increased use of alcohol, prescription medications, or cigarettes. Of course, this can then complicate already disturbed patterns of sleep, appetite, and mood.

In most cases of bereavement, the intensity of the sorrow reaction generally begins to subside after the first months of bereavement, gradually and slowly decreasing in severity thereafter. This is also true among suicide survivors, although remnants of severe sorrow can be present years after the death.

The Initial Reactions Are Grief's Buffer

Initial grief reactions are essentially the same after all types of death. After suicide, however, they seem to endure a little longer than in other forms of bereavement. Thus, suicide survivors may take longer to navigate the initial course of grieving and lag behind on the road to recovery. This fact has led many researchers to differentiate suicide bereavement from other forms of grief. In the words of Samuel Wallace [19], suicide "produces the most intense grieving of any type of death. Whether it be labeled complicated, acute, or any other term, its intensity is searing to the survivor."

In most bereavements, the initial grief reactions of shock, disbelief, and severe sorrow are often accompanied by other reactions such as relief, anger, hostility, panic attacks, a sense of abandonment, and restlessness. These other reactions intrude erratically and are a prelude to the significant and longer lasting reactions that grief embodies. They do not occur as consistently as shock, disbelief, and severe sorrow in the early period of grief. It is against this wide array of other grief reactions that initial reactions buffer the survivor.

When shock and disbelief begin to subside, and before the recovery process has begun, the survivor comes face to face with many emotions. In this book, the emotions that follow the initial reactions to death are called "primary grief reactions."

Calling this complex of troubling emotions and experiences primary reactions is somewhat of a misnomer. In most bereavements, they can be present in the immediate aftermath of the death. They might also exist later in the bereavement when recovery has progressed significantly. However, these reactions typically are more predominant only after shock, disbelief, and severe sorrow dissipate and usually before recovery begins. Therefore, they are referred to here as the primary grief reactions.

Two facts are important regarding the primary grief reactions. First of all, they are always intense and are rooted deep in the psyche of the individual. Therefore, the expression of grief reactions typically involves the whole person. They are not easily, nor without consequence, repressed, blunted, inhibited, nor circumvented. Second, there are few times in any survivor's life when so many different and terribly strong emotions threaten to burst into consciousness at the same time.

Since grief is typically an infrequent experience, its impact is hard to imagine and nearly impossible to passively anticipate. For this single reason, most individuals are not emotionally or psychologically prepared for their encounter with grief.

If the primary grief reactions arose as an immediate consequence to someone's death, the survivor would likely be quickly overcome by their combined intensities. The expected result might well be a breakdown or disintegration of the person on some level, whether it be emotional, physical, psychological, spiritual, or intellectual. However, because a basic motivation to survive exists in all of us, the human psyche intervenes to protect a survivor from the full impact of death.

The psyche protects the person by initiating the shock reaction. Instead of allowing the survivor to be instantly flooded with powerful and frightful grief emotions, shock blunts the response to the intense feelings. It does so to the extent that the survivor is only vaguely aware of the impact of these sensations. Thus, shock gives the survivor time to prepare for the onslaught of the surfacing emotions. It does not usually subside until the person is somewhat ready to deal with them.

Not only does the shock reaction initially blunt and buffer the emotions, it also functions in another manner. As shock wears off, it filters the emotions that arise. This means the emotions do not flood upon the survivor all at once or all at the same time. The survivor usually encounters each emotion in waves, a little bit at a time.

This, in part, explains why the grief reactions often endure longer for survivors of suicide than for other survivors. The greater number and increased intensity of the reactions they experience means the reactions will take longer both to surface and to be resolved by the survivor.

Primary Grief Reactions

Let's emphasize again that grief is an ongoing process. It is not a set of reactions occurring in a given sequence or developing in a fixed pattern of stages. Many of the reactions described as "primary reactions" below, are present immediately in the experience of grief. They are not predominant initially, however, because of the function of shock. Other of these reactions do indeed develop over time as the initial grief reactions subside.

Any and all reactions to death are fully human and natural. They are all perfectly normal, regardless of how common or rare they might be. The primary grief reactions essentially are expressions of emotions that are consequences to a loss.

The intensity of these emotional reactions is directly related to the intensity of the relationship that had been established with the deceased. Consequently, family members suffer a grief more intense than that suffered by friends, who in turn experience grief that is more painful than that suffered by casual acquaintances.

It is critical to the health of the survivor that all, each and every one, of the grief emotions have ample expression. The survivor is likely to find these emotions somehow frightening, but their repression results in further complication of the grief process and later problems of adjustment. In other words, if limits are placed on how much of the grief the survivor deals with, limits will also be imposed upon the level of recovery and readjustment to life she will achieve.

Suicide survivors do not necessarily experience all of the primary reactions described in this chapter. Nor do they experience them in any particular order. Some of these reactions occur consistently among suicide survivors, others are less common. The ones included here are primary grief reactions frequently encountered by survivors of suicidal death.

The primary reactions which commonly surface after shock, disbelief, and severe sorrow weaken their hold on the survivor include preoccupation with the deceased, guilt, anger, depression, loneliness, flight into activity, need to talk, relief, and feeling deserted.

PREOCCUPATION WITH THE DECEASED

Death does not mean that the deceased just suddenly disappears and goes away forever from the life of the survivor. Even after the funeral services and burial, the survivor must deal with the vivid presence of the deceased in her daily life, a presence that goes beyond the mere preoccupation with thoughts and memories of the deceased.

There is a strong instinct within the survivor to, if not regain the lost person entirely, to at least hold on to him for as long as possible. This occurs both consciously and unconsciously. For one thing, memories are very often extremely clear visualizations. The survivor can conjure up in her mind the decedent's face, body, voice, mannerisms, and characteristics no less vividly than if the deceased could physically materialize before her.

The survivor's reflections upon events experienced with the decedent might also take on a clarity which they previously did not have. Past, incidental details are brought to light, as if they had recently happened.

The survivor's dreams of the decedent, rarely about the death itself, can be experienced as real. Dreams are more likely of happier past events or of the often wished for return of the deceased. The survivor is often disturbed upon awakening by the realization that the brief joy of reunion with the decedent was a dream.

It is not unusual for the survivor to search for the deceased. The survivor tries to feel the presence of the decedent nearby or in familiar places. She might maintain familiar routines, like continuing to set an extra place at the supper table, or laying out the decedent's clothes in the morning. In nearly every case of bereavement, the survivor continues to talk to the decedent as if he can still hear and reply. Later, this may take the form of a silent prayer or a brief thought. It seems that this tendency never fully goes away.

Some survivors feel obsessions to go to the same places the deceased frequented. On occasion, she may be startled by the sensation of briefly catching a glimpse of the decedent in a crowd. The survivor might even call out to him, expecting a response.

Often, the survivor believes the decedent will somehow make contact and let the survivor know he is nearby. Many survivors report the actual appearance of the decedent. In these extreme cases survivors might say the decedent's apparition passively observed the survivor, carried a message, performed a task, or engaged in conversation. Survivor's who have this experience describe an encounter so real they are unable to accurately discern whether it happened in reality or in their imagination.

Most survivors spend a great deal of time thinking about the last days of the deceased. It is common among those who witnessed the progression of a terminal illness to painfully recall how the deceased may have suffered or how peacefully he died. Great importance is placed upon whether or not the survivor was present at the death.

Ruminations of suicide survivors especially tend to focus on the moment of death. More so than in other deaths, the images of self-inflicted death seem to capture the survivor's rapt attention.

These images, though conjured up less frequently as time goes by, are likely to retain the vividness of a photograph even years after the death.

GUILT

Guilt is a predominant grief emotion. It is a normal part of any grief and is experienced in several forms. Unless the relationship between the survivor and decedent was somehow seriously disturbed or dysfunctional, these forms of guilt are typically transient and not difficult to resolve as the grief progresses.

Following a death, guilt usually develops regarding events that occurred during the life of the relationship. The survivor often regrets things said or done in anger. She might have a sense of having not done enough to make the decedent's life pleasant. Very often, the survivor berates herself for negligence toward the decedent's needs and wishes. The survivor can exaggerate even minor omissions until they take unrealistic proportions.

Sometimes, grieving persons experience a form of "survivor guilt." This involves a perception that the decedent's death was somehow unfair and that, in some ways, it might have been better for the survivor to have been the one to die.

Finally, guilt can also be a counter-reaction to other natural grief feelings. For instance, feeling anger, shame or relief in regard to the decedent's death often seems inappropriate or wrong to the survivor and results in the experience of more guilt.

Suicide survivors experience much the same guilt as other survivors. They review past interactions with the deceased and sense guilt for acts or omissions which may in some way have disturbed the decedent's peace of mind. They sometimes think they should have died in place of the decedent and they feel guilt over their anger, shame, or relief.

Guilt following suicide is often compounded by the survivor's belief that she shares in the responsibility for the death or that she contributed to it in a significant way. To determine the degree of blame they share with the decedent, suicide survivors commonly analyze the events immediately preceding the death, over and over again.

The survivor frequently thinks she could have or should have done something to prevent the suicide. Some even feel that if it were not for the survivor, the deceased would not have completed suicide. Consequently, the survivor may feel at fault for the death.

Survivors who experience accidents, homicides, and surprise illnesses, also struggle to resolve this guilt of culpability. Yet, for these other survivors of sudden, unexpected death the sense there might have been more that they could have done to prevent the death is typically not as strong as it is for the suicide survivor. They can usually reassure themselves with the facts surrounding the death that they were not responsible for it.

Several factors potentially complicate the suicide survivor's guilt. First of all, suicide usually involves at least two people who are most often engaged in a close, intimate relationship. The deceased has made a choice to end his life, and in a very significant way has rejected the support of the survivor. The implication to the survivor is that she did not make life pleasant enough to make the decedent want to stay alive.

Some survivors perceive the suicide as a revenge for some critical act or omission. In many cases, this may be an accurate assessment of the decedent's intentions. According to Ronald Maris [3], revenge suicides are more prevalent than is usually believed. In other words, many decedent's take their own lives as a way to get even with someone. Apparently, this element of revenge is more likely among younger suicides, high alcohol users, and persons making more than one suicide attempt. The implication of revenge makes it very difficult, if not impossible, for the survivor to exclude her interactions with the decedent from factors that contributed to the suicide.

Another factor compounding the guilt, and contributing to a perception of shared responsibility and fault in the death, is a sensation that the survivor should have known the suicide was going to happen. Maris suggests that many survivors were aware on some level of the decedent's pre-suicidal symptoms or clues, but were either unable or unwilling to intervene in time to stop the suicide. It has become an accepted fact that most, but certainly not all, suicidal persons give many hints, clues, and warnings of their intentions to end their own lives. Edwin Shneidman [7] estimates that as many as 80% of those who complete suicide give clear and definite warnings of their suicidal intentions.

That clues and warnings were probably given, but not heeded, presents a dilemma for the suicide survivor. Only after the suicide does the survivor recall the obvious and subtle ways the decedent was broadcasting his plans to die. As the survivor unearths pre-suicidal warning signs, it becomes increasingly more difficult to detach from responsibility and culpability in the death. It is natural for the survivor to conclude that, if she had paid attention to the decedent's threatened intentions, she would have been able to prevent the suicide.

There are cases of surprise or "blitz" suicides in which the death seems to come out of nowhere and is not preceded by obvious clues or warnings. Even following these, the survivor seems bent on expending a great deal of effort reflecting upon the past, searching for subtle hints of the decedent's suicidal intentions. Quite often the survivor places undue significance upon trivial or minor events.

It is likely that, whether clues were given or not, the consequences remain the same. The survivor will sense that warnings were made, that she should have understood their significance, and that she should have prevented the suicide.

It is important that the survivor acknowledge that pre-suicidal warnings existed, if in fact they did. However, it is equally important to understand that, if the decedent did give clues and warnings, it does not mean the survivor was able, at the time and in the context of their close relationship, to pick up or perceive them for what they were. Survivors are often the last to see warnings or clues because they cared so deeply about the decedent they could not recognize the depth of his pain.

Additionally, even if the survivor received obvious and clear warnings, there is a strong human tendency to believe that suicide will not really be completed. As Ginsburg observes, it is not that persons close to the suicidal individual are blind to his clues, it is simply that they interpret them improperly. Most people do not believe that a person who says that he intends to end his own life will actually do so. This implies that people are likely to ignore or disregard threats mainly because they do not believe them.

Alfred Alvarez believes that "suicide is distasteful to the survivors if for no other reason than that it so effortlessly promotes guilt." While guilt is certainly a common grief reaction in most bereavements, it is a predominant reaction in suicide survivorship. However, although its intensity and complexity contribute significantly to the suicide survivor's bereavement, survivors appear to manage it successfully. They may not resolve the issue of guilt quickly, but most suicide survivors work through the guilt they experience and do not allow it to hamper their recovery any more than do other survivors.

ANGER

An individual experiencing grief generally senses feelings of irritability and bitterness at one time or another. The survivor often may react with impatience, irritability, and anger toward various people during the grieving process.

Feelings like these are frequently part of a pervasive anger that boils within the survivor and quite often bubbles to the surface. Such anger can result in aggressive or irrational behavior that is usually uncharacteristic of the survivor. Although the survivor might have some awareness of an incessant anger toward the decedent or the death, seldom is the anger expressed as outright rage at the decedent for having left the survivor behind.

Anger is a normal result of any significant loss. Death usually means that an important source of satisfaction and gratification has been lost to the survivor. It often means the loss of a source of love, support, companionship, or sexual pleasure. On some psychological level, the survivor may feel the decedent has stolen these satisfactions away by dying, and outbursts of anger may unconsciously become associated with thoughts of him.

Survivors often experience the nagging suspicion that they have been deserted by the decedent. Similar to a child's experience of separation anxiety, a common response to being left behind is anger and temper tantrums.

Anger during bereavement is more than just a response to loss. It also serves a definite function in the process of grieving, for it is significantly instrumental in facilitating the survivor's struggles to successfully separate emotionally from the deceased and to rebuild a life in which he is a missing part.

As is true in other grief reactions, there is often a twist in the anger reaction of the suicide survivor. The heightened sense of guilt and responsibility in suicide, makes it terribly painful for the survivor both to accept that such anger exists and to direct the anger toward the decedent. Denial of anger toward its obvious and rightful object usually results in its expression, with considerable force, upon others.

Samuel Wallace found that suicide survivors often cast irrational blame upon those around them, possibly to forestall the acknowledgement that the decedent made a choice to complete suicide. These survivors commonly rile against officials and institutions rather than directing their anger toward the decedent. Searching for scapegoats, they target their rage against doctors, policemen, coroners, insurance investigators, morticians, and hospital personnel. Other such innocents like store clerks, garage mechanics, or deliverymen may become the targets of the survivor's rage. Although it is helpful to vent anger rather than keep it inside, the unfortunate consequence of redirecting grief anger is that it subverts anger's normal function of aiding in the separation from the deceased.

The inability to express anger appropriately toward the decedent and the death creates further problems. If the survivor directs the anger toward those who would normally want to talk about the suicide, it is likely that the survivor will be alienated from the needed support of others.

Additionally, if the survivor continues to deny the presence of anger, or directs the anger at inappropriate targets, working through the grief becomes more difficult. In such circumstances, anger is blocked in its normal function of helping in the emotional separation from the deceased. It may also preserve the bond with the decedent and allow the survivor to hold on to him for a longer time.

DEPRESSION

Grieving is an internal experience, profoundly subjective and in many ways individualistic. It is often difficult for people, even those who have previously been through a grief, to comprehend the various emotions expressed during bereavement. It is understandable, then, that both the survivor and those around her might be confused about what exactly is happening to the survivor.

Grief is certainly a sorrowful time. One common misinterpretation equates sorrow with depression. Sorrow is not depression, especially in bereavement. After any loss, it would be far more appropriate to say the survivor is grieving, rather than say she is depressed.

The survivor experiences various reactions comprising the process of grieving after a death. Depression is merely a single element, or part, of grief. It is not, in and of itself, the total composition of the grief experience. Genuine depression is a reaction that develops over a period of time. It does not just drop upon the survivor full blown at the outset of grieving.

The depression that develops during grieving might be a consequence, or off-shoot, of several other reactions common to grief. This seems likely because many reactions considered to be symptoms of depression are also inherent to the grief process. These reactions include changes in sleeping patterns and in appetite, dampened emotional reaction, loss of sexual drive, loss of interest in once valued pursuits, suicidal thoughts, anger, and guilt. The combined effects of these normal grief reactions can accumulate and coagulate resulting in the development of the depression syndrome.

Several theories regarding the source of depression have been formulated. One is especially relevant to the explanation of the grief process. This theory maintains that depression develops as a result of a person's experiencing a significant loss.

According to the theory of significant loss, anything with close association to a person acquires importance. This thing can be anything seemingly as trivial as a doll, rock collection, book, or pet, or as major as a person, child, relationship, job, house, or town. Eventually, the important thing will actually be internalized by the person. In other words, the important thing becomes part of the person.

Once an object, possession, or other person has been internalized, it not only feels like a part of the person, but also becomes attached to the person by a bond. It feels much like any other ownership. When a person becomes an internalized part of another, loss of that person is painful to the other because the loss is felt, at least in part, as a loss of self.

The ensuing reaction after loss of the important person is very similar to what happens with infants and young children when they experience separation from a parent. This "separation anxiety" is characterized by a fear that the parent will not return and vigorous outbursts of angry crying. Many times this reaction brings the parent back to the child. When this is repeated often enough, a child learns that having angry outbursts is effective in bringing back a lost object (e.g., a parent).

This is true only if the parent returns to the child. If the child's angry protest at the loss does not bring the separated parent back, the angry protest will eventually subside. Gradually, after occasional tantrums, the child will slip into a state similar to sorrow.

During bereavement, when the initial grief reactions of shock and denial have begun to subside, the death of a significant person is eventually understood to be a permanent separation. At this point, the survivor comprehends that the deceased is physically irretrievable and naturally experiences the pain of losing someone who is a part of herself. The survivor will also feel tremendous anger at experiencing the loss, or more appropriately the snatching away, of something that was hers.

As explained above in the section about anger, grieving people do not, or are not able to, always express the understandable rage that boils within them. According to the significant loss theory, the survivor therefore ends up turning this anger inward. Unable to express the anger openly, the survivor takes it out on herself. She becomes her own target. The survivor becomes depressed. In other words, depression is anger turned inward, against oneself.

Once depression has developed, the survivor can experience many of its symptoms. The most typical is a sense of being sad or unhappy and an inability to overcome it. She may feel hopeless, terribly discouraged about the future, and pessimistic about life. The survivor may be especially critical of herself, finding fault and blame for her actions. She may also be disappointed or disgusted with herself or feel like a failure in life.

Depression commonly includes a sense of guilt or unworth and an impression that one is being, or should be, punished. There may be a feeling of being ugly, repulsive, or unattractive in appearance. A pervasive sense of being annoyed or irritated, uncontrollable fits of crying or loss of all emotion, an oppressive dissatisfaction or loss of interest in all things, and an inability to concentrate or make decisions are all typical.

Fatigue often builds to the point that the survivor finds it difficult to get out of bed or finds it impossible to accomplish any work. There may be increased sleep, an inability to sleep, or different patterns of disturbed sleep.

Depressed people often become more aware and concerned about their physical health, experiencing problems of stomach and headaches, various body pains, constipation and diarrhea. They may also experience a loss or increase of appetite and a weight loss or gain. Loss of sexual drive and interest is common.

Finally, depressed people can experience a loss of will to live or an active interest in dying. They are often prone to accidents and suicide. It is perhaps fortunate that most people who develop severe depression lack the energy and ability to plan in the extreme measure suicide requires. Typically, extreme depression is so debilitating that the person is unable to deliberately take his own life through a single act of suicide. It is actually when the depression begins to lift, and more energy is available, that the risk of suicide increases.

Clinically, depression is usually diagnosed by measuring the presence of any number of these symptoms just described. The presence of any one of these symptoms does not necessarily indicate that depression has developed. In fact, in most cases, depression is more likely when a cluster of symptoms is present.

Many clinicians see depression in a way that is helpful in understanding this grief reaction. They often differentiate between what they call reactive, or acute, depression and endogenous depression.

Reactive depression is typically a response, or reaction, to an external event. A person becomes depressed as a result of something that has happened outside of herself. Endogenous depression, on the other hand, does not require an outside event to precipitate the depression. Here, the depression originates from within the person. Clinicians typically regard endogenous depression more insidious, harder to understand, and more difficult to treat than reactive depression. It often requires professional intervention and drug therapy.

It should be apparent that many symptoms of depression are also common grief reactions. Therefore, it should not be surprising that nearly all survivors experience some depression. In most cases, grief depression is a form of reactive depression. In other words, grief depression is merely a natural reaction to the death of significant person.

For some survivors, depression is a minor reaction of short duration. For others it can be severe and long-lasting. Any depression that becomes chronic, whether it be called grief, reactive, acute, or endogenous, is dangerous. Therefore, chronic and severe depression lasting longer than four consecutive weeks is a threat to the survivor's life and should be treated professionally.

It is difficult to determine if suicide survivors experience a more profound or severe depression than survivors of other forms of death. For one thing, it is difficult to quantify depression and, for another, it is nearly impossible to differentiate natural grief reactions from depressive symptoms. Therefore, there is little research evidence at this time to support even an intuitive inference suggesting that suicide bereavement includes a depressive reaction more intense or longer-lasting than other bereavements.

LONELINESS

It seems obvious that a bereaved survivor would experience loneliness. Most of the survivor's relatives, friends, and comforters make this common assumption. It is a primary motivation for others to keep in contact with the survivor, even if it be infrequently.

As time passes after the death, the survivor often hears comments like "I didn't want you to be lonely tonight" or "Why don't you come out with us tonight so you won't have to be alone." Although some survivors may be sensitive to such remarks and resent them as an intrusion upon their solitude, most survivors respond well to invitations for company and appreciate the offers.

Depending, of course, on the social circumstances of the survivor, loneliness usually dissipates significantly in the later stages of the grief process. This is true especially if other grief reactions have been resolved and recovery from the grief and reintegration into life are underway.

In some, but certainly not all cases, the loneliness of the suicide survivor may follow a different course. Survivors often withdraw into themselves seeking explanations for the suicide. As bereavement continues, the survivor's loneliness can also deepen and intensify as a result of denial, guilt, anger, shame, blame, and depression.

Some survivors unintentionally push would-be comforters away because of the disturbing feelings they encounter after a suicide. In extreme cases they may react with outraged hostility at the offer of company from others. Under such circumstances, comforters are unlikely to persist in their efforts to provide support to the survivor. This might result not only from the hostility and strong emotions they encounter in their interactions with the survivor but also from their own desires to avoid the suicidal nature of the death.

Alienation and isolation of any survivor potentially increase feelings of loneliness and certainly ensure that its impact will endure for longer periods of time than is normal following bereavement.

FLIGHT INTO ACTIVITY

Many survivors, no matter what the cause of death, seem to develop a pattern of restless busyness soon after the death. Typically, this reaction manifests itself within the first weeks of grieving. It is often noticeable as busy work, as moving about in an agitated and purposeless manner, as an inability to sit still, as going about touching familiar things as if exploring them for something, or as a constant push to find something with which to occupy one's self.

There is an irony in this restlessness. As Erich Lindemann points out, all this activity is done with an apparent lack of zest or energy. The survivor just goes through the motions. Even in the flurry of this activity, the survivor experiences a painful lack of capacity to initiate and maintain purposeful, organized patterns of effort. Although she might cling to the daily routine of habitual or prescribed activities, the survivor does so only with tremendous exertion.

The survivor's flight into activity serves a purpose. For one thing, it allows her to avoid, for periods of time, the many overwhelming and disturbing reactions inherent to grief. By keeping busy, sticking to established routines, the survivor unconsciously tries to minimize the significance of the loss. Initially in shock, the survivor hoped to convince herself that the loss did not occur. When the facts and reality of the death cannot be avoided, the survivor tries to prove to herself that the loss did not greatly change things.

Flight into activity is purposeful in another way. At a frightening time when the survivor's emotional life is disintegrating and her psychological stability may be deteriorating, activity is a frantic grasp to hold as much of herself together as possible Thus, flight into activity can be both a form of denial of the importance of the loss and an attempt to regain control of a life that has suddenly been turned inside out.

One common consequence of flight into activity is physical exhaustion. Perhaps unable to sleep, the survivor keeps busy for large portions of the day and night. Eventually, when activity can no longer be maintained, the survivor can collapse into inactivity and sleep. Normally, a cycle of activity and exhaustion temporarily develops. In most cases, the survivor regains a balance between activity and rest in a month or two.

Another potential consequence of flight into activity is a pattern of enduring, chronic hyperactivity. The survivor might learn, consciously or unconsciously, that troublesome memories or thoughts can be avoided by compulsively finding things to do and filling time. Once started, the survivor relentlessly pursues activity. Grieving is blocked and the survivor never slows down.

It is hard to say whether or not flight into activity is more prevalent among suicide survivors than other survivors. It is evident, however, that many suicide survivors do develop patterns of activity that resemble hyperactivity. This might explain the suggestion of some researchers that suicide survivors seem prone to stress-related heart conditions.

NEED TO TALK

The survivor's feelings toward the decedent do not die with the death, and it becomes a major task of grieving for the survivor to work through the feelings that remain for the decedent. This task is facilitated by the survivor's talking freely and openly about the decedent and the death.

The survivor really cannot talk enough about the decedent. In fact, it is healthy for the survivor to talk and talk and talk until she can talk no more. Talking endlessly about the decedent might very well be the best therapy for grief.

This is usually expected of the survivor and readily accepted by those around her early in the bereavement. Encouraging the survivor to talk about the decedent can be the greatest support provided. Comforters often have no more to do than lend an understanding ear. There is little another can say to relieve the survivor's grief anyway.

Unfortunately, as grief continues, the survivor too often encounters people who are uncomfortable talking about the decedent and the death. The survivor inevitably senses this discomfort. Perhaps more sensitive to the other's feelings than the comforter is to hers, the survivor begins avoiding that about which she most clearly wishes to talk. It is in this way the need for talking is often prematurely obstructed. Subsequently, the survivor constrains herself to conversation more acceptable and comfortable to the "comforters."

Something unusual and possibly embarrassing often happens to a survivor who cannot, for whatever reason, talk freely about the grief. Although generally appearing listless and lethargic, the survivor might suddenly engage energetically in conversation about the deceased. The survivor may actually experience a great drive or pressure to talk about the decedent. Words come in a flurry and rush. It appears as if the survivor's conversation has been bottled up. Once uncorked, little can prevent it from gushing forth. This rush of conversation is what psychologists sometimes refer to as "pressure of speech."

Aspects of suicidal death make it crucial for the survivor to talk about the decedent and the death. Certainly, the intensity of the emotional reactions to suicide and the need to explain the death dictate that the survivor will experience a heightened need to talk things through.

The nature of suicidal death often makes talking about the death more difficult than in other bereavements. For one thing, the survivor might have a struggle to break through denial of the realities of the suicide. Avoiding various aspects of the death slows, or prevents, the grief work.

Additionally, most people find it difficult to be open about the kind of feelings usually predominant during suicide bereavement, like guilt, blame, anger, rejection, and shame. Instead of talking out these feelings with another, the suicide survivor sometimes withdraws and isolates herself, trying to deal with troubling emotions alone.

Finally, the likelihood that the survivor will reflect objectively on the life and death of the decedent decreases if the suicide survivor does not talk openly about them. Without shared objectivity, memories can take on powerful proportions and often become distorted.

For suicide survivors, then, it becomes especially important to freely and openly discuss the death with others.

FEELING DESERTED

Nearly all survivors, at one time or another, feel the decedent has deserted them. This may simply be a feeling of being left alone, or left behind. It may also be a sensation of being forgotten by the deceased.

A survivor left with responsibilities once shared by the decedent often experiences strong feelings like these. Any survivor who must continue to raise children, pay off bills, handle financial commitments, or manage a business without the support of the deceased is likely to feel deserted by him.

Additionally, a survivor finding life diminished, unsatisfactory, or overly burdened following the death often holds the decedent accountable for life's changed circumstances. It is as if a day will come when the decedent will have to make it up to the survivor for his unwelcome departure.

Feeling deserted is managed by some survivors with humor. They keep a tally of things they will tell the decedent when they are rejoined. They make oaths to chew the decedent out if they ever catch up with him. They draw the decedent's attention to their triumphs and trials as if he is watching.

Sadly, some survivors react to feeling deserted with bitterness, resentment, and blame. They continue to hold the decedent responsible for various misfortunes long after the death.

The realities of the death usually make it clear to the survivor in most bereavements that the deceased did not choose to leave her behind. Typically, the feeling of being deserted disappears with time. It may resurface later at anniversaries, birthdays, holidays, and special events, but the sensation is fleeting and often times handled openly with humor.

Among suicide survivors, feeling deserted is complicated by the nature of the death. It is harder not to take the death personally if the survivor sees it as the decedent's choice to die. Therefore, the reaction to suicide is usually more than a fleeting sensation of desertion. In fact, suicide survivors often face feelings of deliberate abandonment and rejection.

Abandonment and rejection are special reactions. They will be described in greater detail in Chapters Seven and Eight.

RELIEF

Survivors sometimes feel relieved when a death occurs. This reaction is common when death follows a long-lasting illness, disability, or incapacitation. Death may halt accruing financial difficulties these circumstances usually bring upon families.

Relief is also apparent among survivors who had been involved in a dissatisfying relationship with the decedent. Experiencing relief during grieving is common among survivors who had been in an alcoholic or abusive relationship, who had been in a relationship in which the deceased had suffered from a personality disorder, or who had either already emotionally or physically separated from the decedent.

In all cases in which the survivor senses relief it is likely the relationship with the decedent was in some way an emotionally burden to the survivor. Although the death is painful in some ways, it also lifts the weight of the relationship from her. Additionally, experiencing relief might arouse some guilt for the survivor, but it is more likely to dampen the intensity of other grief reactions and facilitate completion of the grief work.

Suicide survivors do not appear to experience a sense of relief any more or less frequently than others. Certainly, suicide survivors who experience a surprise suicide are not likely to experience any sense of relief unless the relationship with the decedent had been an emotional burden in some other way. It does seem, however, that survivors who were manipulated with previous suicide threats or attempts are more likely to feel relief after the death.

Later Grief Reactions

The grief reactions that have been described are grief reactions suicide survivors share in common with all other survivors. They are also reactions which typically arise early in bereavement. The remaining reactions described in this chapter are also common reactions among all survivors. They are reactions of which the survivor is usually unaware until later in the bereavement.

It is unlikely these reactions would develop early in the grief. They usually result from the cumulative effects of enduring grief. Additionally, they are typically overshadowed by the prominent early grief reactions and are not likely to be acknowledged by the survivor until later. Among the later recognized reactions are loss of self-worth, self-destructive behavior, physical illness, withdrawal and isolation, idealization, and loss of sexual drive.

LOSS OF SELF-WORTH

This reaction to death is closely related to the concept of significant loss described in the development of depression. When we love someone, we form a bond with that person. Unconsciously, we internalize the person, who becomes a part of us. From a psychological standpoint, we become owners of the other person. Loss of the loved person, no matter how it occurs, is also experienced as loss of an important, valued part of ourselves. Lowered self-worth, or self-image, results.

Most survivors experience loss of self-worth during bereavement, especially if the decedent was an important source of support. The survivor is often troubled by thoughts like "What am

I going to do without him," "I can't make it alone," "I'll never be able to do the things he did," or "There will never be another person who could love me the way he did."

It makes intuitive sense, perhaps, that suicide would result in the survivor's loss of self-worth more than any other form of bereavement. Several features of suicide survivorship make loss of self-worth more certain. First of all, the survivor may never be able to fully relieve herself of responsibility in the decedent's decision to perform suicide. This increases the suicide survivor's guilt. Guilt results in lowered esteem.

Second, we commonly resolve our guilts by making atonement or suffering punishment. Since it is difficult to make atonement with the decedent, the survivor may have unconscious desires to seek punishment. Any sense of deserving punishment leads to further loss of self-worth.

Third, the suicide survivor often feels like a failure for not preventing the suicide. Perceiving oneself to have failed in any endeavour results in a reduction of the value one places on one's self. Failure leads to loss of self-worth.

Fourth, the factors leading to a loss of worth are also elements of depression. While depression may be considered merely an element of bereavement, it is also a reaction which results in loss of self-worth. When a person suffers a depression, she also suffers a loss of esteem.

In addition to these four factors, two more complicated factors assault a suicide survivor's self-worth. The first comes from the message suicide carries regarding the survivor's lovableness. As Erich Lindemann and Ina Greer [20] suggest, one way in which we perceive ourselves to be lovable is to believe that the significant people in our lives love us. Implied in this belief is a trust that those who love us will want to be with us and will not deliberately harm, or injure, us.

In an intimate relationship of any depth, our value is somewhat enhanced in our own minds by the belief that the loved and admired person also finds us worthy of his love, friendship, affection, and approval. Therefore, a significant part of our self-worth normally derives from the knowledge that other people find value or worth in us. Self-worth, then, is partly a reflection of what we see of ourselves in the way important people react toward us.

When a significant person performs a self-destructive act, the survivor can not help but take it personally. The implied or obvious message is the decedent did not care enough about the survivor to want to stay with her. In other words, the decedent did not value the survivor enough to choose life with her rather than death without her. The survivor believes the suicide would not have happened if she had possessed any worth in the decedent's eyes. Therefore, the act of suicide devalues the survivor.

The final way in which suicide detracts from the survivor's sense of worth involves social perceptions. Survivors are keenly aware of society's generally poor appraisal of self-inflicted death. They may think, rightly or wrongly, that people look down upon the decedent for performing suicide. The decedent loses value in the eyes of others, and perhaps also in the eyes of the survivor.

Condemnation, whether by society or by the survivor tarnishes memories of the once-valued decedent. Consequentially, a decrease in the decedent's value also decreases any worth she may have placed in the relationship with the survivor. A lowering of the decedent's value means a lowering of the survivor's value. Again, the survivor suffers a loss of worth in self.

Perhaps the clearest example of this last phenomenon is the way suicide is believed to be viewed by a child. When someone significant in a child's life performs suicide, the child may see the act in two different ways. Either leads the child to look upon him or herself as a "bad" person.

In the first case, the child believes the suicide was caused by her own misbehavior. That is, the child made the suicide happen because of her bad behavior. If she had not been bad, the significant person would not have decided to suicide. The child can find ample evidence to make this misperception a fact, since parental suicide has to follow a moment of misbehavior that occurred at some point prior to the act. The child gives her misbehavior incredible power, in fact the very power to kill the parent or to drive the parent to kill himself.

As might be evident, this reaction of children is very similar to the reaction adults experience when confronted by a suicide. However, children do not possess the rational experience or the psychological sophistication adults do to separate their actions from the actions of others. A child, therefore, must often personally suffer the consequences brought about by the actions of others. In this case, the child believes an important person completed suicide because he or she was bad. Seeing one's self as "bad" always results in the loss of self-worth.

The second way a child perceives herself as "bad" is a little more complex. Because of the child's own sense of being cheated by the suicide, or because she senses the uncomfortable or outright negative response of others around her toward the suicide, a child may perceive the decedent as a "bad" person. The decedent did a "bad" thing. Since children do not understand atonement, the child will believe that the decedent must be punished to make up for the "bad" thing he or she has done.

However, the deceased is no longer around to be punished, even by the child's anger. Therefore, through the process called "identification" (described later), the child internalizes the decedent. The child becomes the "bad" person deserving of punishment. Again, perceiving one's self as bad or deserving punishment results in loss of personal value, or self-worth.

Even though adults have greater powers of thought and rationalization than children do, they lose self-worth in much the same way after a suicide as just described. It is often an epic struggle for the suicide survivor of any age to achieve or regain a healthy appraisal of self.

SELF-DESTRUCTIVE BEHAVIOR

Grief obviously represents a major upheaval in the bereaved person's life. Emotional reactions that are part and parcel of grieving can be so overwhelming that the survivor's will to live becomes dangerously blunted on both physical and psychological levels. The survivor's very life may be in jeopardy. For at least a year after a death, all survivors are at risk to take less adequate care of themselves, to become ill, to be hospitalized, to be involved in accidents, or to die or be killed. Arnold Toynbee coined the phrase "peril of survivorship" to describe this phenomenon.

Self-destructive tendencies are often apparent. The survivor might feel, consciously or unconsciously, an overwhelming desire to die. While oppressive thoughts of living without the deceased plague the survivor, she may entertain suicidal ideas. Among all survivors there are those who attempt to harm themselves or take their own lives and those who succeed in completing suicide.

Behaviors not in the best interests of a survivor are not always blatantly self-destructive. All survivors probably go through periods when they do not take adequate care of themselves. Changes in eating, sleeping, activity, and hygienic habits are common during grief. Increased consumption of coffee, nicotine, alcohol, and prescription drugs is also typical. Nearly all survivors who drive are likely to do so, at times, in a preoccupied state of mind, barely aware of any other traffic. In many ways, therefore, the peril of survivorship is a reality regardless of the decedent's cause of death.

The peril of survivorship can be intensified for suicide survivors through another phenomenon called *Identification*. Identification is a psychological term describing how one person takes on characteristics of another person.

A tendency has been observed among many survivors to assume and copy various traits of the decedent. These survivors sometimes begin to mimic mannerisms, facial expressions, nervous tics, verbal expressions, or behavior patterns once characteristic only of the decedent. Survivors might begin to copy attitudes and thoughts previously expressed by the decedent. Survivors have also been known to develop similar physical symptoms if the decedent was ill prior to the death.

An extreme example of identification is expressed by just a few survivors. These survivors report feeling the presence of the deceased within themselves. It seems to them that the decedent's spirit has taken up residence within their bodies.

Identification after death, regardless of its form, is an unconscious attempt on the part of the survivor to hold on to the decedent and to keep him alive. Copying traits of the decedent maintains, in part, his presence. This allows the survivor to continue to unconsciously deny the reality of the loss.

The peril of survival and identification with the decedent compound the risk of self-destructiveness among suicide survivors. For one thing, suicide bereavement is complicated by increased levels of guilt, blame, and responsibility. The intensity and number of grief reactions experienced, the potential isolation of the survivor, her estrangement from society, and her severe demoralization all result in greater susceptibility to self-destructive behavior.

For another thing, identification with the deceased in its ultimate form increases risk of the survivor repeating the suicide experience. Obsessional focus on the suicidal nature of the death often results in the survivor's acceptance of, and identification with, the suicidal act. There are countless examples that illustrate this point.

The number of times identical suicides occur within the same families is an indication that suicide survivors, more than any other survivor, are at greater risk to undertake their own self-destructive course and eventually complete suicide. We need only consider the number of times self-destructive acts are repeated from one generation to the next to understand the power and depth of this risk. A younger brother who drives a car into the same bridge abutment on the anniversary date of an older brother's "accident," a son who takes a gun to his head like his father did twenty years earlier, or a daughter who overdoses on prescription drugs like her mother before her did all serve as examples of identification in its most extreme form.

The insidious influence of identification is also evident among groups of people. The outbreak of "contagious" suicides that periodically plague adolescents in some communities, exemplified by the 1983 Plano, Texas and 1986 Omaha suicides, and "mass" suicides exemplified by the Jonestown suicides are all further examples of the risk of identification.

Identification with the decedent is a very real phenomenon. For some survivors, it is a very real risk. Suicide survivors, especially, must remain aware of, and guard against, identification with the decedent's self-destructive behavior.

PHYSICAL ILLNESS

Physical health concerns are common among bereaved persons. All survivors are likely to believe their general health is not as good as it was before the death. They are more likely to go to a doctor or hospital after a death than they were before it. There is also evidence suggesting a relationship between grieving and an increased risk of dying. In other words, a grieving survivor is more likely to die.

Many illnesses experienced by survivors are believed to include psychological components. Such illnesses are often called psychosomatic illnesses. This label carries negative connotations for many people because it suggests to them that the illness is not real, that it has no physical basis (e.g., germ- or virus-caused), and that it is all in the head of the sick person. Therefore, many people react strongly to being told their physical distress is psychosomatic.

The psychosomatic label does not discount the real physical aspects of illness. Psychosomatic illnesses are considered real and they are known to have physical outcomes. Psychosomatic implies that illness does not always result from purely natural causes and often results from other than physical reactions. In other words, psychosomatic illnesses are physical illnesses often resulting from processes having critical psychological components like anxiety, stress, and depression.

Bereavement is a stressful time. After a death, survivors frequently experience physical symptoms indicative of somatic anxiety and stress. For example, survivors complain more frequently of headaches, digestive upsets, asthma, arthritis, colinitis, and rheumatism, all of which are stress-related. In their situation, it might be more appropriate to identify these physical ailments as "grief-related" illnesses. If it were not for the death, the survivors probably would not be ill.

Colin Parkes [21] reports that people in grief frequently experience heart palpitations and feelings of fullness in the chest. Both of these reactions are typical symptoms of panic attacks and generalized anxiety. Parkes goes so far to say that three-quarters of the increased death rate during the first six months of bereavement is attributable to heart disease, particularly coronary thrombosis and arteriosclerotic heart disease. These forms of heart disease are frequently linked to high, chronic stress levels.

Symptoms of physical ill-health usually develop gradually during bereavement. Naturally, survivors are more fatigued due to sleep loss, reduced appetite, and decreased energy. On top of grief-related symptoms, physical side effects like shaking, nervousness, or intestinal irregularities can result from increased use of alcohol, drugs, tobacco, and caffeinated drinks like coffee. Survivors usually interpret any physical symptom as an incomprehensible deterioration in health rather than rightfully attributing it to the grief process.

Suicide survivors are definitely susceptible to grief-related physical illnesses. Along with physical exhaustion, hyperalertness (or jumpiness), and depression, they frequently report migraine headaches, hypertension, colitis, peptic ulcers, panic attacks, and bronchial asthma.

However, suicide survivors appear no more apt to seek the help of a doctor than other survivors. Nor do they seek the support of a minister, counselor, therapy group, or psychiatrist more often during the grief process than do other survivors.

WITHDRAWAL OR ISOLATION

As described in Chapter Three, artificial limits are commonly imposed upon grief by those who interact with the survivor but who themselves do not experience the full intensity of the grief. Friends, acquaintances, coworkers, or other family members signal the survivor, both directly and subtly, that mourning has lasted long enough. This typically seems to happen two to three months after the funeral.

Survivors commonly report being told "You've got to start getting over this" or "This has gone on long enough" or "He's gone now, you've got to learn to get along without him."

Subtle interference is often encountered also. People begin to change the subject of conversation when the survivor talks about the death or the deceased. Some people become too busy to take telephone calls from the survivor, while others show silent, but obvious, discomfort when she talks about the grief. Any communication suggesting others have had enough of the bereavement, whether directly or subtly expressed, interferes with the survivor's grief work.

Survivor reactions vary when encountering the efforts of others to prematurely bring grief to a close. In order to make the others more comfortable around her, the survivor may put up a front that things are better in her life. She may take part in frivolous conversation, while inwardly crying out to talk about the decedent. Another survivor might demand that others listen, thereby assuring their increased discomfort and the likelihood they will stay away. A survivor might also isolate herself from anyone who seems troubled by or tired of the grief.

Eventually real grieving seems possible only in solitude or with someone who is patient and understanding. In nearly every case, the time arrives when the survivor must complete much of the grief work alone.

Any bereavement, regardless of the cause of death, results in some amount of loneliness and isolation. Since few people are comfortable listening to the survivor talk about the death, support for the survivor typically diminishes noticeably after the official mourning period. There might be changes in relationships with family members, in-laws, and friends. Friendships developed within the context of the relationship with the decedent are often lost or abandoned. The survivor sometimes feels less socially likable and often feels like a fifth wheel or tang-along.

Factors common to suicidal death increase the likelihood of lost social support and isolation among suicide survivors. For example, it is common for suicide survivors to hesitate or avoid talking about the death. It is also characteristic for some suicide survivors to isolate themselves in order to cope with guilt, anger, shame, and the perception of stigma associated with suicide. On the other hand, some friends may deliberately avoid the survivor.

The general distaste for suicide often results in decreased availability of support normally offered to survivors. A large segment within our society views suicide as a shameful act bringing embarrassment and stigmatization to those close to the decedent. Kjell Erik Rudestam [22] reports that nearly half of the people asked about a relative who had died by suicide did not want to discuss the event. Nearly one-third sometimes hedged about the death, describing it as an accident or natural death.

It is clear that friends and family often insist that the survivor not talk about the death. They may even argue vehemently that the death was not a suicide. They might also direct considerable blame for the suicide toward the survivor. Greater withdrawal or isolation under circumstances such as these is understandable.

IDEALIZATION

Understandably, it is the good parts of the relationship with the decedent, however little there may have been, that the survivor will miss most of all. Memories of what was good and pleasant to the survivor have special meaning. Therefore, it is natural that the survivor's attention and preoccupation will predominantly focus upon this significant aspect of the loss.

For mourning to be successfully completed, the survivor must attain a realistic perception of the decedent's humanness, faults and all. It sometimes seems, however, that the survivor clings to memories of the decedent's finer qualities, that remembering unpleasant parts of the relationship is somehow threatening. Of course, every survivor has memories of the decedent's faults, failings, and weaknesses. There seems to be a natural tendency to avoid them, though.

Admitting to unpleasant parts of a relationship can be an arduous task. In part, the guilt, remorse, and anger with which the survivor is already struggling contribute to this difficulty. Acknowledging negative aspects of either the decedent or the relationship often increases the intensity of these troubling emotions.

Unpleasant memories regarding the decedent are also often repressed at a deep psychological level. It seems unfair and disloyal to talk about anything but the pleasant memories. This repression is suggestive of an ancient psychological taboo against speaking ill of the dead.

Honest consideration of all aspects of the relationship and characteristics of the decedent becomes more likely as grief progresses. Troublesome emotions are slowly resolved and the survivor's psychic energy begins to replenish. At this later point, the need to defend against ill thoughts toward the deceased usually begins to diminish.

If a survivor's guilt and emotional pain regarding the death are severe enough, she tends to continue avoiding negative thoughts about the decedent. When a survivor feels safe recalling only good aspects of the relationship, the deceased can become idealized in the survivor's perception. This is similar to being granted "sainthood."

There is little seriously counterproductive in elevating the decedent's status unless the idealized image, devoid of human frailties, is internalized by the survivor. Unfortunately, internalization of an idealized image creates a scale against which the survivor will make future comparisons of herself and others. Since the internalized ideal image presents an impossible standard to be measured against, the scales of comparison tip heavily in favor of the idealized decedent. Later, the survivor may discover increasing difficulty accepting common human faults within herself and others. Ultimately, the grief process can be thwarted and recovery, as might be demonstrated in the formation of healthy and rewarding new relationships, is less likely.

Suicide survivors do not necessarily idealize the decedent but they often do find it hard to acknowledge his human faults. The survivor's wish to deny the truth regarding the suicidal circumstances of the death contributes significantly to this difficulty.

The culturally-determined negative judgement regarding suicide makes it nearly impossible for the survivor to consider the suicidal act as anything but "bad" or abnormal. When an act is considered bad, there is a natural inclination to consider the one who performs it bad also. Therefore, to judge suicide bad is also to judge the decedent bad.

This puts the suicide survivor in a tenuous and unenviable position. Denying the suicidal nature of the death and avoiding negative thoughts about the deceased lead to, and reinforce each other. This circular reaction prevents honest appraisal of the relationship and the deceased. It also nearly guarantees unfinished grief work.

The difficulty suicide survivors face in acknowledging unpleasant memories can also be attributed to the greater intensity of guilt and anger reactions they often experience. Consideration of the decedent's failings can be dangerous because it invariably results in an intense surge of additional guilt.

In terms of current learning theory, the survivor experiences this guilt surge as a sort of punishment for thinking less than good thoughts about the decedent. To avoid these punishing sequences the survivor expends a great deal of energy to avoid negative thoughts about the decedent.

Attempting to avoid further guilt in this way prevents seeing the decedent's humanness honestly and accepting it in its entirety. As just suggested above, a likely result is that the grief process will be short-circuited and the survivor will be stuck in grief. Ultimately, denying the nature of the suicidal death and avoiding the articulation of anything but fine and glowing remarks about the decedent can continue throughout the remainder of the survivor's life.

LOSS OF SEXUAL DRIVE

Bereavement brings with it a disturbing upset of human appetites. The survivor's characteristic needs, urges, and drives, and the behaviors expressive of them, are torn and scrambled. A survivor may find it impossible to go to sleep or may sleep for long periods of the day and night. She might be unable to eat or might endlessly devour food with no interest in what is being ingested. The survivor might also become compulsively hyperactive or might be paralyzed by lethargy and listlessness. Similarly, survivors are commonly assailed by uncharacteristic sexual appetites.

In some instances, the individual is troubled by sexual stirrings erupting as early in the grief process as during the funeral arrangements. Some survivors report experiencing an acute sexual longing early in the bereavement, but it is usually a temporary reaction.

Acting upon sexual longings sometimes develops into a pattern of promiscuity. More than a desire for sexual fulfillment or satisfaction, this may be a way for the survivor to avoid the pain of grief. Excessive sexual activity early in bereavement might also reflect the survivor's needs to bolster diminished self-image, to instill hope for a satisfying future, and to vent anger, hostility, and aggression.

In contrast, an almost complete blunting of sexual desire and drive can develop as bereavement progresses. Considering the number and intensity of emotional reactions suddenly confronting the survivor, it is not remarkable that her sexual libido would be drained. In fact, such reactions to grief like psychic numbing, shock, and depression almost always have the impact of lowering sexual desire and expression.

Survivors often fear they have become frigid or impotent. This is rarely, if ever, the case. As grieving progresses, most survivors usually recognize a rekindling of sexual drives. As sexual feelings revitalize, however, it is not always easy nor feasible to act upon them.

This certainly seems true of some suicide survivors. After a suicide, many survivors experience a loss of trust in themselves and in other people. Fear of intimacy often develops and endures for long periods. Consequently, loss of trust and fear of intimacy can blunt both the drive to engage in sexual activity and the capacity to perform such activity.

How soon into the grief process the survivor is able to engage in characteristic sexual activity depends greatly on the efficiency of the grief work. If emotional reactions are dealt with and resolved, sexual drives and desires usually return little changed from their state prior to the death. For some survivors this may occur within a few months. For others, however, years might pass before the critical grief work is com- pleted and sexuality can be expressed normally.

Suicide Bereavement Is More Than Common Grief

In large part, suicide bereavement is the same as other bereavements. The grief reactions described in this chapter are normally experienced by all survivors, regardless of the cause of death. As common grief reactions, they also comprise a significant part of suicide bereavement. If they are different at all within suicide bereavement, it is in the intensity with which they assail the survivor. Evidently, some grief reactions, like guilt, which are not typically serious in other bereavements, may reach severe levels within suicide bereavement.

As suggested earlier, there is more to grieving a suicide than is common in other bereavements. The suicide survivor also experiences special grief reactions resulting from special aspects of death by suicide, such as its unexpected nature, the fact that death occurs by other-than-natural cause, and the all too evident fact that the death was self-inflicted. The special reactions encountered by suicide survivors are described in the following three chapters.

CHAPTER SIX
Because Suicide Can Be So Unexpected

"While it may not be possible to say that one kind of loss is more painful than the other, the trauma of unanticipated loss is clearly the more disabling."

Colin Parkes & Robert Weiss [11]

Suicide is sudden and unexpected death. Even when previous suicide threats or attempts are experienced, most people do not believe death will occur by suicide. Very few suicide survivors are prepared for death, let alone a suicidal death.

Death is certainly traumatic even when anticipated. Yet, knowing in advance that a death is probable or imminent gives the survivor time to prepare for the trauma. It seems to help the survivor understand it. It also allows her to begin redefining both her concept of self and her life apart from the decedent before the death actually happens. Anticipation, therefore, is an important determinant of the survivor's ability to accept the death and to achieve recovery.

In contrast, Parkes and Weiss maintain that survivors of unexpected death often dwell on what happened and search desperately for reasons to explain the death. They conclude that unanticipated death, regardless of its cause, results in the most severe bereavement reactions.

Unexpected death occurs in many forms, including accidents, homicides, suicides, heart attacks, renal failures, tumors, hemorrhages, and other natural causes. In addition to common grief reactions following any loss, survivors experiencing sudden and unexpected death must also deal with special grief reactions. These special reactions are not usually encountered by survivors who have anticipated the death.

Since suicide is usually swift and unanticipated, unexpected grief reactions are common additions to its bereavement. Of course, these special grief reactions are not unique to suicide survivors. They are shared by most survivors traumatized by unexpected death, regardless of its cause.

Grief reactions which result from unexpected death include an extended search for an explanation, taking responsibility for the death, feeling blamed for the death, vivid memories of the time of death, and resultant dysfunctional relationships.

SEARCH FOR EXPLANATION

To accept death, it is important there be an acceptable reason for it. Thus, when death occurs, nearly all survivors initially question why the deceased was taken from their lives. The strength and plausibility of available explanations influence the severity and length of the grief experience and determine whether or not the survivor will be able to make sense of the loss.

Religious explanations for death seem most likely. For example, accepting death as "God's will," believing God has brought the decedent home, that he rests in God's arms, or has achieved a final reward in heaven are common explanations.

Philosophical explanations answer the question of death for some survivors. Examples include "Death is just the final stage of life," "He is better off away from life's trials," and "Death comes to each of us in our own time."

Additionally, simple rational explanations are often enough to provide the survivor understanding for the death. Examples include "We are all human and must eventually die," "He would never have wanted this to happen," and "Those left behind have to pick up the pieces and go on with their lives."

Grief is not an expression of concern for the decedent. It does not result from a belief that the decedent is suffering in death or is worse off for having died and left life behind. Grief is a process of dealing with a loss to self. The pain of grief is that an important part of the survivor's life has been completely and irretrievably snatched away.

The search for explanation is an effective outlet for the "self-pity" normal in bereavement. Realistically, the search for an acceptable answer to the decedent's death is more a search for an answer to the survivor's suffering such a painful loss.

Among survivors prepared for death, the search for an explanation is usually not a serious concern. It does not occupy a major portion of the survivor's attention and is commonly resolved early in bereavement. In part, this is because these survivors suffer through a portion of their grief and resolve some of their self-pity before the death. Also, the survivor may take time prior to the death to reach acceptable reasons for it.

Unexpected death results in a search for answers that is more intense, more solitary, and more difficult to complete than follows anticipated death. Common explanations, whether religious, philosophical, or rational, are not so easily accepted when death comes swiftly. For one thing, survivors unprepared for death deny its reality for longer periods of time than those expecting the death. For another, sudden death often appears to have been preventable to the survivor. Consequently, accepting any answer for their own suffering takes a longer time and a harder course.

Among suicide survivors, looking for reasons for the death is a significant and critical grief reaction. It occupies a great deal of the survivor's time, energy, and attention. It can go on for years after the death, and sometimes is never satisfactorily resolved.

Part of the survivor's difficulty is that the search for explanation after suicide is invested with guilt. As described in Chapter Five, these survivors often encounter a more intense form of guilt than other survivors. Their search for explanation, therefore, is not just a search to answer why the loss to self must be suffered. It is also, in large measure, a scrutiny of the relationship to determine how much responsibility she shares for the suicide.

Search for explanation is made all the harder because of the nature of suicidal death. The decedent chose to die. Neither the survivors nor those who seek to comfort them can disregard the self-inflicted element of the death. The question "Why?", apparently on everyone's mind, becomes pervasive and overwhelming. The questions seem far weightier than the possible answers, and the survivor is often left to discover what answers she can alone.

The explanations for death usually shared among mourners and comforters do not fit the circumstances as well. There is little comfort for suicide survivors in remarks like "It was God's will," "He is happier now with God," "It was meant to be," "His time had come," "There was nothing more you could have done." All seem inappropriate and are seldom offered.

There have been cultures in which explanations for suicide were socially acceptable. In several eastern cultures, if a person intent on regaining his honor performed suicide, it was considered a noble act. Romans no longer able to maintain a pleasant, productive, or dignified life, were free to end their lives without moral, legal or religious condemnation. Norsemen who had grown too old or infirm to fight or who had become social burdens performed acceptable and noble suicide. In our own culture, soldiers who knowingly sacrifice their own lives for the sake of comrades-in-arms are rendered honored memorials.

In the circumstances of normal, day to day living, however, suicide is generally not accepted in our society. There are no romantic Romeo and Juliet suicides nor noble Socrates suicides. Today, suicides are tragic and blameworthy, and someone must be held accountable when they happen.

The particular circumstances surrounding each suicide may be different, but most people consider suicide simply an escape from some intolerable circumstance. The most common explanations for suicide include fractured love relationships, personal problems, disappointed expectations, financial difficulties, depressions, humiliations, hopelessness, long-endured pain or physical illnesses, and mental illnesses. These explanations for death obviously differ from those society offers other survivors. They are not comforting and the survivor usually does not find them emotionally acceptable.

Those who have not experienced a suicide may not comprehend the difficulty faced by suicide survivors in arriving at an acceptable explanation for the death. Explaining why a person decides to end his or her life takes time and emotional effort. Typically, the survivors begin the search by dissecting the events and interactions that took place with the decedent just before the death. They consider these most likely to have precipitated the suicidal act and give these events a special power that is not ordinary. Survivors also tend to focus on omissions of actions they may have taken to change the decedent's mind.

Although "precipitating events" are overemphasized and laden with mythical qualities, they almost always prove to be inadequate explanations for the suicide. On a rational level, no one really believes a person decides to take her own life because angry words were spoken, a meal was burned, a date was forgotten, a bank account was overdrawn, the car fender was dented, a lover left without a kiss goodbye, a promotion fell through, or any of the other myriad reasons often considered to explain suicide. The survivor seldom finds an acceptable reason among them.

As Karl Menninger [23] says, "What is characteristic of a very large number of suicides is the apparent inadequacy of the precipitating event [as an explanation for its occurrence]." Since precipitating events usually do not satisfactorily answer the question "Why?", the survivor must look elsewhere for the solution.

Usually a painful reflection of historical events in the life with the decedent follows. In other words, the survivor looks for past failures shared with the deceased. Events perhaps years old are subjected to microscopic analysis, all too frequently resulting in sad, and usually unwarranted, conclusions. Many a survivor berates herself with remorseful ruminations like "If only I had...," or "If only I had not..."

Looking to the past seldom yields satisfactory answers for the survivor, either. The problem is the survivor cannot be detached enough from the relationship to see the facts clearly. Also, few survivors are able to separate their interactions with the decedent from the entire span of the decedent's life course. They do not look far enough into the decedent's past to discover where the roots of the suicidal death likely lie. Consequently, survivors tend to accept responsibility for the suicide.

Few suicides result from a singular, acute life crisis or event. As William Steele [24] states, there is no one reason why a person takes his life. The feelings that bring a person to a suicidal crisis result from a series of losses and difficult times. It is the combination of losses and failures that brings most people to the conclusion that life is not worth living.

Suicide is a very complex, multidimensional act that develops over the course of a life-time. Karl Menninger suggests that the self-destructive tendencies take root very early in a person's life and so strongly influence the entire course of development as to overshadow and finally conquer the opposing instinct to live.

Menninger maintains that suicide is an extremely complex reaction to life. It cannot be viewed as a simple act of impulse, whether the act be considered logical or irrational. Nor can suicide "be explained as the result of heredity, suggestion, [insanity], or any of the other symptoms of maladjustment which so frequently precede it. Rather, we are frequently able to see the steady progression of self-destructive tendencies first appearing long before the consummation of the critical act."

Similarly, Ronald Maris suggests most individuals who die by suicide have historically made self-destructive adaptations to life's circumstances. He points out that suicides tend to have greater accumulated developmental burdens and stresses than people who do not complete suicide. Maris considers suicide a product of gradual loss of hope and the will and resources to live. It is a kind of running down and out of life energies, a bankruptcy of physic defenses against death and decay.

Realistically, interactions between survivor and decedent are only peripherally implicated in any self-destructive act. The real causes and motivations for suicide are internal and develop throughout a person's life. This helps explain the difficulty of devising satisfactory explanations for the decedent's action after the suicidal event.

Explanations for suicide are to be found only within the individual who chooses self-destruction. According to Alfred Alvarez, "each suicide has its own inner logic and unrepeatable despair." No matter how intimate the relationship, no one is privy to the inner workings of another's emotions, thought processes, and unconscious drives. As Menninger rightfully concludes, an understanding of the motives to complete suicide is made difficult not only because the motives that seem obvious are most untrustworthy but also because "a successful suicide is beyond study."

The difficulty involved in the suicide survivor's search for explanation, the search for the "why" of an individual suicide, is succinctly summarized by Edwin Shneidman [25]. He states the "causes of suicide are multiple and terribly complex and remain one of the great enigmas of human nature."

Ultimately in the survivor's search, there will be no real "explanation" for why the decedent completed suicide. The reasons are always hidden within the decedent and, therefore, lost forever in the act of self-destruction chosen. Explanations can not be derived from the analysis of every day interactions or isolated events.

The hope for the survivor is that she will, as much as possible, relieve herself of any burden of responsibility and accept the suicide as a choice made alone, for whatever reason, by the decedent.

TAKING RESPONSIBILITY

When death happens unexpectedly, there is a nagging perception that it could have been prevented, avoided, or somehow postponed. Very often, it is the survivor who takes responsibility for not preventing the death.

Survivors of unexpected death assume undue responsibility for the death in several ways. The most troubling for any survivor is the perception that she somehow directly caused it. Another is the belief that the survivor could have or should have prevented the death. There may also be a sense that the survivor should have been aware that death was imminent instead of being surprised by it.

Perhaps more than any survivor of unexpected death, the suicide survivor is likely to experience an overwhelming sense of responsibility in the decedent's death. The survivor may feel that she drove the decedent to despair or desperation. Nearly all feel they should have at least been aware of the decedent's suicidal intent and acted to prevent the death. This is especially true if the decedent had ever communicated suicidal intent.

The idea of shared responsibility for suicidal death is rooted in social attitudes. As previously noted, our culture offers no adequate or acceptable explanations for death by suicide. The survivor usually searches independently for reasons and is likely to discover ways in which she appears to be responsible for the suicide.

Suicide survivors usually focus on personal actions or minor omissions which appear to have motivated the decedent's self-destructive act. As Goldberg and Mudd [26] suggest, the self-inflicted death is often hostile and loaded with the implication the survivor is somehow at fault. The survivor, after the fact, finds it almost impossible to ignore this accusation.

Cultural beliefs generate further difficulties for the suicide survivor. Current social attitudes stress that suicides can be and should be stopped. In other words, if a suicide could have been prevented, it should have been. This pervasive attitude places the responsibility for suicide prevention outside the decedent. This means the responsibility for the decedent's action lies with someone else.

As Ginsburg states, many people believe the responsibility to see that suicide attempts do not occur or recur lies particularly within the family. Therefore, there is a greater tendency among suicide survivors to take responsibility for either causing the death or for not preventing it than is likely in any other bereavement.

The difficulty with attitudes and beliefs that place the responsibility for suicide outside the decedent is they disregard the inherent realities of self-destruction. These beliefs essentially ignore facts that many in the suicide prevention profession have recognized. The truth about suicide is that, when a person decides to take her own life, fully intends to die, and has the lethal method at hand, there is little to nothing another person can do to prevent that particular suicide. Also, if a person has given up all hope for life, she will evade every effort to save her life and take the first opportunity to bring it to an end.

If there is doubt about this, it is illuminating to consider Ronald Maris's contention that 75% of those who complete suicide do so in their first attempt. Is it because the survivor didn't respond to the crisis quickly or efficiently enough that so many people successfully end their lives, or is it because the decedents' intent to die is strong enough that they select a time and method for their death in which intervention is impossible? *Time Magazine* (July 17, 1989) reports that 64% of the men and 40% of the women who killed themselves in 1986 did so with firearms. Of the 464 gun fatalities reported in the week May 1-7, 1989, 216 (47%) were suicides. Some of these individuals shot themselves in the presence or close proximity of other family members. The use of a gun in a suicide strongly implies the finality of the action. Lethal methods like guns usually remove the chance of a life-saving change of mind, discovery, or rescue--even when those who might stop the suicide are present.

The true responsibility for the suicide lies with the decedent, not the survivor. If this fact evades the survivor, the consequence of the generally-accepted social belief that suicide should be prevented is likely to be that she can never, with any great assurance, conclude whether or not her actions might have made a difference in the completion of the other's death.

74

There is another feature of assuming responsibility for the death few survivors, other than suicide survivors, experience. It is likely associated with searching for an explanation. It is the importance of clues.

Most suicide survivors search for clues that might have indicated before the suicide that it was going to happen. Most discover them, both obvious and subtle. With clues uncovered, survivors castigate themselves for not being sensitive enough to notice the clues in time and do something about them.

Unfortunately for the survivor, this hindsight is given far too much power. For one thing, the relationship between the survivor and decedent is usually too close for the survivor to be able to perceive a clue for what it is. For another, even if the survivor might have been acutely aware of the decedent's suicidal potential, only in exceptional cases does a survivor believe that a suicide will occur. Most individuals, regardless of the seriousness of the circumstances, can not anticipate self-inflicted death nor believe it might happen.

Clues certainly occur. However, their authority in predicting a suicide is mythical. We all experience in our interactions with others many of the clues that "predict" suicide. It is not unusual to encounter others who are depressed, hopeless, despairing, or unusually euphoric, who give their prized things away, who say strange goodbyes, or who write troubling or confused notes or letters. In most cases, such clues are not followed by suicide and they hold no particular significance. We think little of them in retrospect.

It is only in hindsight, when a suicide has occurred, that clues aggregate their demonic power. The belief in clues serves no helpful purpose for the survivor. Ultimately, this belief serves only to increase the survivor's tormenting struggle to be relieved of responsibility in the death.

FEELING BLAMED

"If it weren't for you he'd still be alive!" Sudden death in our society seems to imply that the decedent was in some sort of stressful or frustrated state, and attitudes toward the death and the survivor are sometimes judgmental or punitive. This is true whether the death was by natural cause, accident, homicide, or suicide.

When death comes unexpectedly, shock to both the survivor and others around her is intensified. An early need in the bereavement is to assign a causal explanation for the death in order to make sense of the loss. As described above, it is more difficult to understand and accept unexpected death. Also, responsibility for the loss is assumed by the survivor.

These reactions to unexpected death result in the survivor feeling blame for the death. Troubling enough as it is, the survivor also often encounters obvious blame from others. Such outright blame for the death usually comes from family and friends of the deceased.

Casting blame is probably the consequence of a need to find a "scapegoat" for sudden death. Someone must be at fault when a person suddenly dies without a warning.

The survivor does not necessarily encounter blame to feel blamed. Normal guilt, need for an explanation, and taking responsibility, can all result in the survivor feeling blame-worthy. Sensitivities like these make the survivor vulnerable to misinterpret remarks, facial expressions, and gestures of others. The survivor then might naturally assume others consider her at fault, whether they do or not.

Feeling blame increases the suicide survivor's burden of grief unnecessarily. Just as it is not appropriate to assign the suicide to a single cause, it is not appropriate to assign blame for the death to anyone but the decedent. As Edward Dunne and Karen Dunne-Maxim [27] state, it seems inappropriate to single out and blame any other person as the agent of a suicide, whether it be a parent, sibling, spouse, lover, friend, or therapist. They give responsibility for the suicide to no one but the decedent. In their words, "the failure to choose life is the failure of the deceased, not of the survivors."

Blame, whether blatant, implied, or imagined, is one bereavement feature unexpected death survivors experience almost exclusively. There is little evidence at this time to indicate if blame is intensified for suicide survivors beyond that experienced by other unexpected death survivors. It is safe to say, however, that experiencing blame in some way for the suicide is a common and consistent aspect of suicide bereavement.

VIVID MEMORIES OF THE DEATH

All survivors have memories of things that occurred at the time of the death. Such memories usually include the day, date, time, and place of the death. Most survivors also very clearly remember where they were and what they were doing when they learned of it. As time passes, some memories fade. Years later, for example, the survivor may be less clear of the date or not think so much of the time the death happened.

How vivid such memories of the death remain is partly determined by several factors. These include the circumstances surrounding the death, anticipation of the death, and whether or not the survivor was present at the death.

Survivors present at an expected death that occurs by natural cause and in which the decedent did not suffer painful or traumatic complications are least troubled by vivid recollections of the moment. If the death was difficult for the decedent, even the memories of expected natural death can be vivid and enduring for the survivor. Memories of the time of death are also complicated for these survivors if they were informed of it afterwards instead of being present for the death.

The moment of being told of the death is frequently recalled as if captured on a photograph. Survivors remember the surroundings, the sight, smell, feel, and sound of that moment, in clear detail long years after the death.

The memory of the time of death does not fade as readily among survivors of unexpected death. Among suicide survivors it does not seem to fade at all.

Unexpected death survivors are not usually present when the death occurs, rather they are informed of it afterwards. The memory of that event, of being told the death has taken place, is likely to be imprinted vividly upon the survivor's mind. The shock of it fixes the details of that moment into sharp contrast with the "every-day" events that preceded it. For years afterwards, especially around the anniversary of the death, the survivors are likely to experience vivid recollections of being informed of the death. When they describe the details of that event, it is as if it had just recently happened.

There is an additional element to this reaction that some accident survivors and nearly all suicide survivors experience. Not only does the time of death become a vivid memory for these survivors, the memory of it also assumes painful and troublesome proportions.

Troublesome memories seem most frequent among suicide survivors. This is especially true of survivors who were witness to the suicide or who found the decedent's body. Some experience difficult memories as frequently as daily or weekly.

There are suicide survivors who become nervous, anxious, depressed, sad, or somehow agitated every day at the hour coinciding with the time of death or of being informed of it. Others become uneasy weekly on the day the death occurred, for example, every Saturday afternoon.

Suicide survivors also report difficulty in returning either to the place where the death happened or where they were when informed of it. This strong response to the death often means the survivor will move to a new locale immediately. Some are never able to go back into the house, walk into the basement, sleep in the bedroom, or go out to the garage if that is where the suicide occurred. There are also survivors who quit jobs or request transfers because they are unable to feel at ease in the place they were informed of the death.

Many survivors find these vivid memories so painful and disturbing they expend great efforts to avoid them. Typically, such efforts imbue the memories with even more emotional power and make them all the more threatening when the survivor can no longer keep them shut out.

The impact of unexpected death and the added characteristics of suicidal death make this event in the survivor's life one of the most traumatic a person might ever experience. Remembering the moment of death or of being informed of it can elicit strong emotions from the suicide survivor years after the death.

78

DYSFUNCTIONAL RELATIONSHIPS

A "functional" relationship is one which fosters the emotional, spiritual, psychological, mental, and physical welfare of one, or both, of the individuals involved. It ultimately functions to enhance the person's well-being and survival. A functional relationship "works" to the advantage of the persons who invest in it.

In contrast, a "dysfunctional" relationship is one which, in some important way, does not foster the person's healthy development. It works against the person, discouraging, detracting from, and undermining his or her healthy and balanced well-being.

Bereavement is a transitional state of existence. It is a period in which the survivor moves from being the person she was in relationship to the decedent to becoming the person she will be having lost a significant part of herself. While grief progresses, changes in the survivor's relationships are frequent. Some relationships are strengthened. On the other hand, grief can tax and threaten any relationship, whether it be with a family member, friend, or work associate. How relationships weather the storm of grief depends, in part, on how the survivor transits her bereavement, on the quality of the relationship before the death, on the personality of the survivor, and on the understanding of the other toward the survivor.

A suicide survivor brings intense grief reactions into her relationships. Otherwise comfortable relationships can be stressed and challenged to the breaking point as the survivor copes with anger, guilt, depression, blame, feeling responsible, and trying to explain the suicide. A troubled or conflictual relationship can be expected to come apart at the seams as sparks turn into major fireworks.

There seems to be a greater tendency for survivors of unexpected death to experience dysfunctional relationships compared with survivors having had an opportunity to prepare for death. This may be a result of the basic difference in the two bereavements. Survivors expecting death have time to prepare for the loss of the relationship. Preparing for the death includes anticipation of the loss of satisfactions and gratifications of the relationship. When the death occurs, the shock of its loss is not quite as devastating, and the survivor does not cling so desperately to the relationship.

Whether or not her relationships survive the bereavement, generally the survivor eventually returns to thinking, behaving, and feeling in ways similar to before the death. There is a part of the survivor, of course, that will never be the same. That is the part that had been shared with the decedent.

How significant is the part of self lost after a death can depend, in part, on how individualized the survivor was within the relationship with the decedent. This, in turn, can affect how long grief endures. A survivor who had been very dependent upon the decedent will take longer to complete the grief work than a person who had been able to achieve and maintain some level of independence and individualization within the relationship.

Spouses, lovers, and partners are especially at risk for developing dysfunctional relationships after a suicide. Understandably, survivors of sudden death experience strong urges to fill the empty spot left by the death. They also, quite naturally, desire to escape from or to be rescued from the painful complex of emotions grief brings. Some survivors respond by replacing the lost relationship with a new one. In fact, unfulfilled needs sometimes "push" the survivor to seek out new relationships during bereavement.

Relationships, even those that have been established before the death, are a risky business at this time. As stated above, the survivor is going through a transition. She will not return entirely to being her former self nor can she know who she will become when the grief process has been completed.

Unexpected death is a sudden and cruel severance of a relationship. It is like stripping away living flesh from the survivor's frame. One way to anesthetize the pain of such loss is to replace the lost relationship with another. Unfortunately, relationships developed within the first year or two of bereavement are usually founded upon unhealthy psychological complexes. These factors primarily operate on an unconscious level well beneath the survivor's awareness, and interfere with her perceptions and judgments.

Most survivors are incapable of objectively perceiving the state they are in while deluged with grief's strong emotions. Thus, the survivor is not likely to be in a psychological state facilitating beneficial and satisfying choices. Relationships that don't work for the survivor are likely. Many, but not all, relationships formed during this period are neither functional nor long-lasting and seem doomed to flounder.

Frequently, relationships established during bereavement follow somewhat predictable patterns. Sometimes the survivor involves herself with someone who seems remarkably similar to the decedent or with someone who seems the complete opposite. Other survivors involve themselves in repetitious relationships. Each of these is fraught with emotional difficulties.

A relationship with someone apparently similar to the decedent can present problems. The new relationship is not really a replacement of the old relationship, it is more a continuance of it. This seems to reflect a tendency on the survivor's part to select a person in whom the old complaints and problems of the prior relationship are repeated. Thus, the new relationship is at once an old and familiar one, grounded in part by an unconscious wish not only to have the decedent back but also to deny that the death ever happened. It is as if the survivor says to herself, "See nothing is different. He's still here. Nothing has changed. He's not dead."

Survivors probably form relationships with a person unlike the decedent to facilitate separation from the decedent. Subconsciously, the survivor concludes a person unlike the decedent might help her to avoid thinking about the decedent. This relationship becomes a defensive repression of grief.

Large adjustments are required in forming any new relationship. Doing so with someone unlike the decedent, almost ensures that adjustments will be continuous. The survivor will be faced with countless comparisons which threaten to return the focus back upon the deceased. This can make adjustment within the new relationship confusing. Continuous adjustments of this sort also steal away from the time, effort, and energy that would better be directed toward completing the grief work. Incomplete bereavement and a troubled relationship are often the result.

The dynamics of repetitious relationships are somewhat complex. The example provided by multiple marriages may make it more understandable.

Those who have observed multiple marriages have discovered that a survivor of one marriage often selects someone who is "just like the first one" for a second or third partner. This is especially apparent in alcoholic marriages. It is not uncommon that one marriage to an alcoholic, severed by death or divorce, is followed by another.

The choice of a "carbon copy" partner is determined by unconscious motivations and decisions. In other words, the survivor forms the relationship without actually knowing or understanding why. The substitution of one alcoholic partner for another indicates, in part, that the grief work consequent to the loss of the first relationship was incomplete. Repetitions occur because the reactions to the original loss, and the personal issues operative in the relationship, were not adequately resolved by the survivor.

As defined above, dysfunctional relationships are those that do not work well for the survivor. Alcoholic relationships are one example; grief-stricken relationships may be another.

One danger exists among suicide survivors that other survivors of unexpected death seldom face. Similar to some survivors of alcoholic dyads, a small number of suicide survivors tend to substitute the decedent with another suicidal person. This substitution might reflect an unconscious attempt to relieve guilt for omissions in the relationship and for failing to prevent the suicide. In essence, the survivor tries to relieve herself of responsibility for the first suicide by saving another suicidal person from completing a self-destructive course.

In this light, relationships suicide survivors develop while grieving are potentially rescue missions. The survivor's objectives in these missions are to atone for past failures and to affirm her worth and goodness. The survivor proves to self and others that she was not at fault for the first suicide.

Some suicide survivors experience a series of brief and fruitless relationships, resembling push-pull contests. The survivor desires and needs intimacy, actively courts it, but then draws back from it in fearful alarm. Other survivors isolate themselves and avoid relationships altogether. Both patterns result from a fear of the loss of love and a fundamental loss of trust.

Experiencing or expressing feelings of love while suffering emotional pain is difficult. Some survivors interpret the normal loss of loving feelings during bereavement as an inability to love and worry that the condition is permanent. Proving this fear unfounded often underlies the motivation for entering new relationships.

Many suicide survivors report feeling a loss of trust, not just in others, but loss of trust in self as well. The survivor questions whether she can trust another person not to do the same thing the decedent did. She also questions her own judgement, her ability to make choices so apparently flawed and terribly blind in the previous relationship. She believes, if only for awhile, that she would not have been involved in a relationship ending in suicide if she had been able to judge others adequately in the first place.

Some survivors are fortunate enough to build new relationships that help in completing the grief work. Usually, these survivors have already accomplished much of the grief work before entering the relationship.

Generally, suicide survivors would be well-advised to refrain from romantic involvements in at least the first year of bereavement. Unless the survivor is uncommonly lucky, trying to find intimacy and satisfaction in new relationships tends to be troublesome and largely unsuccessful while grief reactions are unresolved and still in process. Milestones of the grief work must be encountered openly and overstepped successfully. Only after grief's transitional state is eclipsed, only after the survivor is the person she will be apart from the decedent, are fulfilling and prosperous relationships probable.

CHAPTER SEVEN
It Didn't Have To Be This Way

"It is as though the person who commits suicide puts his social skeleton in the survivor's psychological closet."

Edwin Shneidman [25]

Death can be divided into a number of categories. The last chapter presented information dividing death into expected and unexpected death. Now death will be separated into natural and other-than-natural causes.

Two million Americans die each year. Natural causes claim most of these lives. 1,860,000 deaths result from biological, organic, or physical causes like illness, disease, infection, and organ failure. 140,000 (or 7%) of the total annual deaths result from other-than-natural causes. These untimely deaths include accidents, disasters, homicides, and suicides.

Survivors experience special grief reactions when death does not result from natural causes. Accident, homicide, and suicide survivors all deal with these special reactions in some degree, whereas survivors of natural death, whether expected or unexpected, seldom experience them.

At the root of these reactions is the belief among other-than-natural death survivors that the death did not have to happen. Deaths occurring by other-than-natural cause present the survivor with a dilemma. Unlike survivors of natural death who can explain, rationalize, and justify the death without great difficulty, other-than-natural death survivors are likely to be confronted by an awareness that, had circumstances been somehow different, the death would not have happened.

Accident, homicide, and suicide survivors can be plagued by this dilemma for long periods of time throughout the bereavement. The grief reactions resulting from a belief that the death did not have to happen add to the suicide survivor's bereavement and are hard to resolve.

The special other-than-natural grief reactions described in this chapter include viewing the death as preventable, feeling stigmatized by the death, and feeling the decedent deliberately abandoned the survivor.

PREVENTABLE DEATH

Natural death, even when it occurs suddenly, has a quality of being inevitable. Death from commonly fatal causes, like serious illness, disease, or organ failure, are more understandable for the survivor. Death by cancer or heart attack does not usually present the dilemma of preventability. Even though some physical illnesses certainly result from the decedent not taking proper or adequate care of herself, most natural deaths seem largely unavoidable. Most survivors accept that little beyond divine intervention could have prevented the death.

Other-than-natural death survivors consistently view the death as somehow preventable. Accident, homicide, and suicide survivors all express the belief that the death did not have to happen, that it was not inevitable. Believing the death to have been avoidable adds an "if only..." quality not often found among natural death survivors.

Thoughts and statements of other-than-natural death survivors reflect this quality. Frequent examples include, "If only he had not gone out that night," "If only I had called him," "If only he hadn't been there," "If only I had stopped him from leaving," "If only he had waited," "If only it had not rained," or "If only he hadn't bought that gun."

Believing the death to be preventable is especially apparent among suicide survivors. The self-inflicted nature of suicide makes it nearly impossible to see the death as anything but preventable. Suicidal death seems preventable in the extreme because it is controlled by a deliberate act of the decedent.

Accidents and homicides may seem beyond the victim's control. Survivors, therefore, are often able to rationalize the death as strictly circumstantial, that is, the result of external factors or fateful circumstances. Suicide survivors, on the other hand, seldom consider the death circumstantial, and their grief is imbued with an intense "if only" quality expressed in the singularly troubling statement, "If only he had not killed himself!"

Believing an individual's suicide preventable often becomes an obstacle to acceptance of the death and resolution of the grief. The "if only" quality of the death is difficult to work through, and survivors tend to expend a great amount of grief energy puzzling over it. Combined with the search for the "why" of the suicide and the survivor's sense of culpability, the "if only's" become an entangled mess that slows the grief process down considerably in its early stages. Along with the "whys," the "if only's" are likely to plague the survivor for many years after the suicide.

STIGMA

The word "stigma" comes from an ancient Greek and Roman practice of burning marks into the skin of criminals and slaves. A stigma was a token of disgrace, reproach, or infamy. It indicated a person's status and was considered a visible character reference. The branding mark gave significant and easily recognizable information about the person's character to others unfamiliar with him.

Today's application of stigma has changed only in the fact that a person stigmatized is not actually subjected to physical branding. A stigma today burns a person emotionally, psychologically, or mentally.

Stigmatization results in a person feeling somehow scarred or marked in a negative or unpleasant way. As in times past, a stigma retains the power to detract from or to permanently damage the reputation of the person to whom it is given.

Survivors of naturally-caused deaths seldom experience a sensation of being scarred or marked. Accident, homicide, and suicide survivors, on the other hand, frequently must deal with the additional grief stress of stigma.

Among suicide survivors, being stigmatized by the death is linked to social beliefs and attitudes. Stigma seems to be a psychologically projected and a mentally perceived mark of shame rooted in society's tendency to blame and hold someone accountable for suicide. No less than a murderer might be stigmatized for a death committed at his hands, suicide survivors sometimes sense themselves marked by the decedent's self-destructive act. The unfairness of this sensation is the suicide survivor, unlike the murderer, has had no real hand in the death.

Stigma is closely associated with events that occur after the cause of death is apparent. Mark Solomon [28] describes events that can result in a survivor's feeling marked by suicide. These include encountering gossip, blame, social avoidance, and unpleasant public contacts.

Suicide survivors are frequently aware of gossip about the death, sometimes of an insensitive nature. Some survivors are blatantly accused of responsibility for the suicide, especially when a suicide note blames the survivor for the death. The survivor may also feel avoided by friends or family. Some among the survivor's contacts may stubbornly refuse to acknowledge the suicidal nature of the death and rather talk of it as if it were an accident. A conspiracy of silence sometimes develops in which both the topic of death and the suicide are generally avoided.

Finally, suicide survivors sometimes find contacts with officials abrasive or unsympathetic, or discover the suicide sensationally reported by the media. Such are the experiences that tend to elicit feelings of shame among survivors.

Many people look upon suicide as a shameful death. Ginsburg studied public conceptions and attitudes toward suicide in the Reno, Nevada area. A large number of people interviewed believe suicide brings shame, disgrace, guilt or responsibility for the death upon the decedent's family. Ginsburg concludes a pall of stigma is cast over both the decedent and the survivor after a suicide, and he believes the resulting sense of social disgrace is a significant torment within suicide grief.

Not all suicide survivors experience stigma. In fact, Mark Solomon suggests only one-third believe themselves to be stigmatized by the suicide. He also concludes stigma is not overly troublesome among those who do encounter it. Solomon adds that potentially stigmatizing events are neither necessary nor sufficient in themselves to result in stigma.

Nearly three-quarters of the survivors Solomon interviewed had encountered at least one negative event and one-third reported encountering several of them. Only 18% of the survivors experienced no stigmatizing events during their grieving.

Interestingly, some survivors who experienced none of the stigmatizing events still sensed the sting of stigma. On the other hand, some survivors who experienced many negative events did not feel stigmatized by the suicide.

Solomon notes survivors most likely to feel stigmatized by a suicide are also those likely to have encountered many more negative events than survivors who do not feel stigmatized. This suggests stigma, if encountered at all, results not from any particular negative event, but from an accumulated effect of experiencing a number of negative experiences after a suicide.

DELIBERATE ABANDONMENT

Feeling deserted by the decedent was described as a common reaction among all survivors in Chapter Five. The sensation of being deserted seldom implies any deliberateness or intentionality on the part of the decedent, however. Therefore, it usually is not an intense or troublesome reaction to death. The grief of many other-than-natural death survivors generally includes a reaction going beyond this feeling of desertion.

Other-than-natural death survivors frequently feel deliberately abandoned by the decedent. This reaction is probably associated with the apparent preventability of these deaths. Unlike desertion, deliberate abandonment implies an "on purpose" motive on the part of the decedent. Intentionality might seem especially evident in certain circumstances, for example, when a death occurs after the survivor and decedent have had a disagreement.

If the deceased walked out on the survivor during an angry argument and was killed in an automobile accident, the survivor may unconsciously believe the decedent deliberately walked out and "left" the survivor on purpose. Death feels like a purposeful leaving.

Among most other-than-natural death survivors, the feeling of deliberate abandonment loses intensity as bereavement progresses. As grief emotions subside, the circumstances of the death are viewed more realistically, and survivors can accept that the decedent did not deliberately intend to die.

The self-inflicted nature of suicide makes it difficult for suicide survivors to disregard intentionality in the decedent's motives. Suicidal death is more than just a choice to die. Many times it is interpreted as the decedent's choice to leave the survivor. Suicide survivors confuse the decedent's intention to die with an intention on his or her part to leave the survivor, even though the two are not the same thing. Suicide survivors, then, frequently experience feeling deliberately abandoned by the deceased and they typically have a more difficult time resolving this special grief reaction than do other non-natural death survivors.

This reaction will be discussed in greater detail in the next chapter's description of rejection.

CHAPTER EIGHT
No Other Survivor Could Imagine

"Suicide is simply the most extreme and brutal way of making sure that you will not readily be forgotten."

Alfred Alvarez [8]

Grief reactions common both in suicide bereavement and in other forms of grieving have been described in the previous three chapters. The description of grief reactions experienced by suicide survivors ends in this chapter with a discussion of reactions uncommon to any other but suicide bereavement. Although these particular reactions are present in other forms of bereavement, they are rare among most survivors. [Research among the growing number of survivors experiencing AIDS-related death might alter this fact.] Thus, the presence of such reactions during bereavement is strong indication the death was suicidal.

Rare reactions certainly are not experienced by all suicide survivors. However, they occur consistently, frequently, and often intensely enough among suicide survivors to be significant and powerful deterrents to successful resolution of grief. The existence of these rare and special reactions has led many researchers to view suicide bereavement as unique. In a sense, because they happen so infrequently among all other survivors, these reactions may well be described as unique to suicide survivorship.

It should be evident from the presentation in the preceding chapters that there is more to suicide bereavement than just these rare reactions. Suicide survivorship is largely comprised of a complex of grief reactions "normal" in other bereavements, also. The grief reactions special and unique to suicide account for a small, but important, part of the survivor's experience.

Included among the special grief reactions that might be viewed as unique to suicide survivorship are denial of the cause of death, a sense of rejection by the decedent, embarrassment regarding the death, a fear of insanity, the death as a moral issue, and communication problems.

DENIAL OF THE CAUSE OF DEATH

Each person in our society decides what to think about the act of suicide, and most people develop a bias against it early in childhood. Young children know about suicide. They understand it is the act of killing one's self. They talk about suicide, think about it sometimes as a way to get back at parents, and sometimes threaten it when they are angry. Children also learn such an act is unacceptable, frightening, "wrong," or "bad."

During adolescence, young people frame the concept of suicide within more rigid, moralistic views. Usually, by the time a person reaches adulthood, attitudes about the "wrongness" of self-destruction are well ingrained. Suicide, then is typically seen as distasteful, repugnant, abhorrent, sinful, selfish, hateful, or evil.

The negative view of suicide is so deeply ingrained that, for most people, considering it an alternative is terribly difficult even in the most trying of times. In this way, negative beliefs about suicide serve as prohibitions against it.

Suicide survivors are as likely as any other person to have developed negative feelings toward suicide early in life. When they experience a suicide, therefore, they run headlong into their own biases against it. On a psychological level, the survivor deals with suicide, and feelings about it, in one of two ways.

First, the survivor can accept the suicidal nature of the death. This also permits him to continue to accept the decedent as a "good" person. Second, the survivor can reject suicide in some moral or negative sense. In this case, it is harder for him to accept the decedent, and the survivor often ends grief by rejecting the decedent instead. After a suicide, the survivor is challenged to separate feelings about the actions of the de- cedent from feelings about the decedent herself.

These two choices present the survivor with a "dilemma of resolution." Accepting the decedent is experienced as accepting suicide. Rejecting suicide is experienced as rejecting the decedent. This dilemma is especially apparent among survivors who had been involved in a close, satisfying relationship with the decedent. It is hard to both accept the decedent and the self-inflicted death. Survivors who do not reject the decedent out-right must deal, then, with their feelings and attitudes about suicide. This is the dilemma of resolution.

Realistically, rejecting or accepting suicide is not a simple matter. Morally rejecting suicide is a natural, ingrained tendency. The survivor discovers, however, that rejection of the decedent on some conscious level usually follows. Most suicide survivors do not reject the decedent. The struggle then becomes one of accepting the decedent on one hand while rejecting the self-destructive act on the other.

One way the suicide survivor solves this dilemma is to accept the decedent without dealing with the suicide. Denial of the cause of death is a common way to escape dealing with suicide. For example, a suicide survivor might say the cause of death was something other than suicide, referring to the death as an accident, heart attack or organ failure.

Denial of the suicidal nature of the death is hard to maintain, unless the cause was equivocal. For one thing, denial is easily shredded by facts surrounding the death. For another, denial requires zealous effort, resulting in a heavier emotional burden for the survivor. To strengthen their defensive denial of the cause of death, survivors often stoke it with hostility and anger. Consequently, then, denial of the suicidal nature of death can lead to incomplete grieving or chronic hostility and anger.

The suicide survivor can solve the dilemma of resolution in another way if no doubt exists about the circumstances of the death, and the survivor does not deny its cause. He does so by reframing his beliefs about suicide. The survivor makes continued acceptance of the decedent easier by viewing suicide in less than negative terms. In other words, the act is rationalized in more positive ways than it had been before the death.

Thus, some suicide survivors end the dilemma by seeing suicide as an acceptable way of dying. This does not mean these survivors think about suicide for themselves. Acceptance implies only a more philosophical view of self-inflicted death. The survivors let go of judgmental views of suicide and no longer think of it as wrong, repugnant, aberrant, or sinful.

Overcoming a prejudice against suicide and accepting it as a way of death is a Herculean task. Survivors usually struggle with denial of the cause of death for some time. They waver between the ingrained rejection of suicide and the efforts to somehow accept it.

Some survivors never completely resolve this dilemma. They hold on to strictly negative attitudes toward suicide. Their acceptance of the decedent after completing the repugnant act is, therefore, marked by ambivalence, anger, and frustration. Holding on to both rejection of suicide and acceptance of the decedent makes for an arduous task.

Among survivors who had been involved in difficult, conflictual, or burdensome relationships, the dilemma might not arise. If the survivor rejects the decedent as not a worthwhile person, he can easily hold on to negative attitudes toward suicide. Consequently, the survivor rejects both the decedent and the act of suicide with little change in attitudes toward either.

Denial of cause of death makes suicide survivorship different from any other bereavement from the start. No other survivors deal with the cause of death with such painful effort. No other survivors must so completely reconcile both the death itself and its cause. Such reconciliation is an important part of most suicide bereavements and, if the dilemma of resolution continues, the survivor's bereavement is often prolonged.

REJECTION

Feeling deserted and deliberately abandoned have been described as parts of other bereavements. Among suicide survivors, sensations of this nature take on more serious and enduring proportions. In fact, beyond feeling deserted or deliberately abandoned, suicide survivors might experience the death as an outright and intentional rejection by the decedent.

Rejection might be somehow implied or inferred in other forms of death. In suicide, rejection is determined by a very specific act performed by the decedent. After a suicide, survivors find it difficult to define the act in any other way than as a rejection. It appears there are few suicide survivors who do not experience the death in this way.

That suicide survivors commonly feel the decedent chose to leave them or rejected them, clearly and consistently distinguishes suicide bereavements from others. Most suicide survivors feel rejected by the decedent, while few other survivors experience any degree of personal rejection.

Charles Neuringer [29] concludes suicide is unique among the ways of dying because of the strong message that it carries to the survivor. The suicide makes a statement about the feelings that were shared between the decedent and survivor. The conscious deliberateness of purpose in the act intensifies the survivor's impression that he was deserted because the shared feelings were inadequate.

Some survivors actually see the death as the decedent's revenge upon them. Suicide survivors frequently feel the decedent was somehow getting even with them by dying. Although this might seem just a "paranoid" reaction by the survivor, in some cases such feelings might be valid. Karl Menninger [23] suggests the decedent often kills herself for the express purpose of taking revenge upon the survivor. The resultant feelings of rejection and abandonment experienced by the survivor are almost always inherent in the self-destructive act itself.

That suicide communicates a message of rejection may carry beyond the immediate relationship with the close survivor. As Robert Kastenbaum [30] suggests, the person who completes suicide seems to flaunt society, hinting that the kind of lives we have built for ourselves are not worth keeping. The person rejects sanctions against suicide, thereby assaulting the social fabric that ties all of us together as humans. Perhaps it is this assault, this apparent indictment against our lives, that makes suicidal death so generally troublesome to most of us. Even so, the survivor remains the one who deals intimately with the rejecting aspect of suicide. As Kastenbaum concludes, more than rejecting a way of life, the decedent rejects the option to share in the love and the life offered by the survivor. It is the survivor who bears the brunt of the decedent's rejection.

EMBARRASSMENT

Bereaved survivors usually do not feel embarrassed by the death of another person, unless that death happens to be a suicide. Feeling embarrassment is a rare reaction to death and is largely unique to suicide survivorship.

Suicide survivors frequently say that admitting to a suicide within the family is accompanied by shameful feelings. They feel acknowledging the suicidal nature of a death also implies something about themselves. Survivors also tend to feel other people look upon them in a less than favorable light after the suicide.

Social attitudes toward suicide are at the root of this reaction. Many people believe something is terribly wrong with anyone who completes suicide or that something is wrong somewhere in her life. The suicide survivor is as likely as anyone else to embrace this belief on a deep, psychological level. Consequently, the survivor naturally thinks others have made a judgement against the decedent.

Assuming the judgments of others based on our own internal perceptions is called "projection" in psychology. In this case, survivors project their own beliefs onto others; that is, because they believe something must have been wrong with the decedent, they assume others will think the same thing.

One troubling consequence of projection is experienced by survivors who consider suicide evidence of insanity. This shame-filled view of suicide combined with the survivor's projection of beliefs can result in the following illogical thinking: "Anyone who completes suicide must be crazy; my _____ must have been crazy because she took her own life; if others find out she completed suicide, they'll think she was crazy." Some survivors follow this nonlogic with a question. "If they think she was crazy, will they think I'm crazy too?"

The embarrassment or shame suicide survivors feel creates more difficult social interactions than otherwise normal during grieving. Suicide survivors typically experience discomfort in revealing the cause of death. Conversations with casual acquaintances or strangers fill survivors with anxiety that the secret of the suicide might somehow come to light. Some survivors tell people the death was an accident. Others are vague when discussing the circumstances of the death. In extreme cases, suicide survivors avoid talking about the death, or even bringing up the decedent's name, altogether.

The survivor's embarrassment often leads to strained social interactions or avoidance of contact with others. Therefore, more than any other survivor, the suicide survivor might deliberately stay away from people who could be helpful in resolving the grief.

FEAR OF INSANITY

Many suicide survivors experience anxiety or fear of losing their own sanity. This is not surprising, since most survivors are unfamiliar with the intense emotional reactions common to suicide bereavement. Feeling suddenly uprooted, untethered, or uncontrolled is extremely disquieting. Additionally, any survivor is likely to be troubled by his behavior if grief is expressed through uncharacteristic acting out of anger, hostility, or sorrow. Momentary thoughts like "I'm going crazy," "I'm losing my mind," "I can't stand another minute of this," or "I'm losing all control" are common.

Compounding an awareness that behavior and emotions seem to be beyond control, depression verging on despair usually develops as the grief process progresses. The future might seem empty of any hope or promise for the survivor. Doubt that life will ever again be rewarding or satisfying grows. To the survivor, the world becomes an unsafe place in which the rug can simply be yanked from beneath him at any moment. The survivor's trust in the goodness of life vanishes.

In the face of such pervasive hopelessness and amid the fear of lost mental control, a survivor is sometimes besieged by thoughts of his own suicide. This might be the first, and only, time the survivor has ever seriously entertained vivid self-destructive thoughts. Under these traumatic developments, the survivor naturally fears he will be unable to prevent the completion of his own suicidal ideas.

Finally, a large segment of our population believes the myth that people who perform suicide are mentally ill or psychologically unbalanced. Although less than 15% of those who kill themselves are considered mentally ill, fear that the decedent was mentally unstable, or momentarily deranged, may lurk somewhere in darkened corners of the survivor's mind even if he has been able to unearth a plausible explanation for the suicide. Any fear that the decedent really was "crazy" can be twisted into a similar fear that the survivor is a little insane, also. Fears like these feed upon underlying anxieties that suicidal behavior is contagious or runs in families, and they are heightened by the survivor's own suicidal thoughts.

Understandably, fears and anxieties about the survivor's own mental and psychological stability become an addition to the burden of suicide bereavement.

THE DEATH AS A MORAL ISSUE

Scriptures do not specifically address suicide, nor pronounce a judgement upon it. The moral injunction against suicide has not been passed by the lips of God, but by the condemning voices of men inferring, assuming, or perhaps presuming, to know the mind of God on this matter.

St. Augustine (354-430) was alarmed by the number of Christians who zealously sought eternal glory by actively courting or bringing about their own deaths. Augustine spoke out against suicide in his comments to the Church, exhorting the end of self-inflicted death. The Church finally responded in 533 AD by defining suicide as the deadliest of mortal sins.

Labeling an unacceptable act a sin might increase the guilt associated with performance of that act, but it has never fully deterred people from indulging in the "sinful" act. Therefore, labeling suicide a sin has never been the deterrent Augustine may have hoped it would be. It has, however, added significantly to the suicide survivor's burden in resolving grief.

Most of the legal statutes declaring suicide a crime have been removed from active law or have long been ignored. Those who attempt suicide are seldom legally degraded, fined, or prosecuted. Unfortunately for survivors after a suicide, the same cannot be said of the Christian injunctions against self-inflicted death. The Church, although more sensitive to the trauma of survivors, has not revised its position on the sinfulness of suicide.

The Church's traditional opinion on self-inflicted murder was that the victim had no opportunity to atone for the act, thereby negating any chance of God's forgiveness. The victim surrendered her life and condemned her soul to damnation.

Only suicide survivors deal with moral considerations of the cause of death. They worry about the state of the decedent's soul and often seek reassurance from clergy members that the decedent has not been damned to hell. This reassurance is difficult to obtain, not because the clergy is unsympathetic, but because survivors are so aware of the Church's traditional stance on suicide. They do not find it easy to forget the "deadliest of mortal sins."

Moral and religious concerns are hard to resolve. Real answers are nonexistent, at least in this life. Many survivors carry their worries for the decedent's soul with them for the rest of their own lives. Others choose to rely on God's mercy and benevolence and, thereby, let go of this particular worry.

COMMUNICATION PROBLEMS

A realistic and honest acceptance of circumstances surrounding a death is the foundation of healthy grieving. Additionally, successful completion of any bereavement is influenced by the opportunity for the survivor to talk openly and honestly about grief. When a survivor is not able to be honest about the circumstances surrounding the death, grieving is inhibited.

Only among suicide survivors are communication difficulties regarding the death common. Emotional grief reactions, like denial, shame, guilt, and stigma, typical in suicide bereavement, make dealing with the suicide hard and retard the survivor's communication of grief.

For example, denial the death was suicide can be so strong the survivor vehemently and, many times, violently confronts anyone daring to suggest the death was self-inflicted. Open hostility like this sometimes extends even to those attempting just to talk about the death.

Some survivors insist the death was accidental, even when obvious evidence betrays the suicide, like when a note reveals self-intended death. Depending on how vehement is the survivor's denial, the discomfort of people intending to console the survivor may be increased. Already without socially approved and "proper" condolences to extend to the suicide survivor, the comforter may be further confused at encountering hostility. Both survivor and comforter find expressing themselves openly difficult, and each might seek to avoid the other, alienating the survivor further.

Some survivors, shamed beyond tolerance, distort or deliberately conceal the truth about the death. This happens especially in families with surviving young children. Sometimes adults insist the cause of death was natural, even when the child is aware of the self-destructive act, as would be the case if the child witnessed the death or discovered the body. Adults often do not allow children to talk about the death or demand they keep its cause a secret from others.

Children are confused by such experiences. They learn that talking about death is to be avoided, or that, if it is talked about, it is not done so in frank or honest terms. Children also learn from this to distrust perceptions of reality, both their's and other people's important to them.

An excellent example of disruption of open communication is often observed among fathers of adolescent suicides. Some fathers display outrage and hostility toward anyone wanting to talk about the death. They may adamantly insist the death was an accident and rage if the death certificate is signed as a suicide. The difficulties these fathers have in dealing with suicide is worthy of sympathy. A young person's suicide seems particularly troubling and abhorrent. In fact, Pamela Cantor [31] suggests grief reactions common within suicide bereavement may actually be further accentuated with the suicide of a young person.

The inability to talk openly and honestly about suicide is common throughout our society. The difficulty this presents to survivors can have enduring effects. If survivors cannot find a forum in which to discuss the suicide, communication problems intensify and grief stalls.

Chapter's End

This chapter concludes the description of grief reactions typically experienced by suicide survivors. Clearly, bereavement marked by so many reactions places the survivor in a vulnerable position. The complex interaction of any number of such intense reactions often results in a difficult grief experience for the survivor. The ways suicide survivors manage their bereavement and the grief outcomes that might be expected after a suicide are the topics of the next chapters.

CHAPTER NINE
The Aftermath

"We who have come back, we know: the best of us did not return."

Victor E. Frankl [32]

Any survivor would be comforted by the assurance that complete recovery from grief and reconstruction of a satisfying life will be accomplished two years after the death. Grief is too inconsistent in expression among individuals to be predictable in course, however. Projecting ahead is impossible.

Survivors grieve in different ways. The manner in which one person might experience grief is determined by the interaction of various factors. John McIntosh [33] includes among the most important of these factors the family relationship between survivor and deceased, the survivor's social support network, individual personality and coping abilities, emotional attachment or closeness to the deceased, and the ages of both survivor and deceased.

Factors That Influence Grief

The type and quality of relationship lost by the survivor dramatically influence the severity of grief. Bereavements differ among survivors who are spouses, parents, children, brothers, sisters, uncles, friends, lovers, work associates, or casual acquaintances of the decedent. The quality of the relationship, whether it was pleasant, hostile, shallow, intense, satisfying, painful, growing, or deteriorating at the time of death, further affects the experience of grief. For example, a wife who enjoyed a pleasant, growing, and maturing relationship with the decedent experiences a grief different from a wife who had a painful, destructive, and deteriorating relationship.

Many characteristics of the survivor affect bereavement. These include age, personality features, life experiences, prior grief experiences, faith, attitudes, beliefs, and reality perceptions.

Generally, then, a survivor's personal attributes partly determine intensity and duration of grief reactions.

Personality development continues throughout a person's life and reflects his life-long experiences. However, the foundation of personality is laid in childhood and adolescence, long before involvement in adult relationships. Among adult survivors, therefore, reactions to death will mirror individualistic and characteristic responses typical of the survivor in past stressful situations.

For example, a person might characteristically become hyperactive and anxious when under stress. Such primary responses to stress are also likely to be predominant during bereavement. They also tend to overshadow other grief reactions. Thus, this survivor's activity and anxiety might be obvious, while his guilt, fear, loneliness, and preoccupation with the deceased are little noticed. Unfortunately, little regarded grief reactions become little resolved reactions.

Circumstances surrounding the death are clearly significant in determining the course of bereavement. As explained in previous chapters, the survivor's reactions to the death are influenced by whether the death was of natural or other-than-natural cause, whether it was expected or came suddenly, and whether it was unintentional or deliberate. Death that is not expected or by natural cause usually brings with it additional grief reactions. In fact, the more troublesome the circumstances of the death for the survivor, the greater will be the number and intensity of grief reactions.

Finally, circumstances after a death contribute to the bereavement process. Life in the aftermath of death is different for each survivor. For example, among survivors who lose a marital partner, financial stability and security vary. Some have to return immediately to work, change jobs, or find work for the first time, whereas others remain at home, quite jobs, or take extended leaves of absence. If the survivors are parents, they may find the level of conflict elevated in their own marriage, or the death may bring them into a closer relationship with each other. Some survivors initiate a move to a new residence or locality (itself a major stressor) and others stay entrenched where they had been before the death.

The circumstances into which a survivor is thrust after a death not only have important effects upon bereavement, they also highlight another fact. After a death, survivors quickly discover life does not halt while the grief work goes along. In fact, the pace of life often accelerates in many ways.

Survivors learn that channeling emotional energy exclusively into grieving is not possible. At times, grief must be set aside while survivors attend to changes in their lives. Most survivors are gradually able to refocus there energies away from grieving for longer periods. Fortunately in this regard, the distress of grief does not continue unabated until it is finished.

Survivors are not always bundles of raw, exposed nerve endings. Even in the worst of the grieving, survivors are blessed with calm moments when the intense and overwhelming "grief pangs" are dulled. Thus, depending upon circumstances after the death, grief usually shares time and focus with concerns for children, family, finances, jobs, school, careers, and with moments of calm, peace, and genuine laughter.

How Long Does Grief Last?

Successful resolution of grief depends upon how honestly the survivor acknowledges grief reactions and how diligently he works through them. The survivor must expend time and effort in doing so. Frequently and understandably, survivors often wonder how long their grief will continue.

We should be cautious about assigning specific time limits to bereavement. Studies of grief indicate that grief's duration varies from one survivor to the next, depending on many of the factors just discussed. Some survivors perform the grief work relatively quickly, apparently completing the grief process within six months of the death. In contrast, other survivors grieve for the remainder of their lives. Generally, however, survivors complete the grief work over a period of years.

Despite such variabilities, enough commonalities exist among survivors to permit some *generalizations* about how long grief endures. For instance, few survivors finish their grief within the first year after the death. Grief typically progresses through two to four years.

The intensity of principle grief reactions usually declines significantly between the first and second years of bereavement. Grief is not completed at this point, however. Survivors continue to feel some degree of loneliness, psychological discomfort, social isolation, and impaired physical health. Survivors also tend to view the world as an insecure, hostile, and unsafe place during this time.

Grief is largely resolved by the fourth year of bereavement and, although some elements of grief linger, survivors are usually well into recovery by this time. Some survivors have brief moments of crying, longing, loneliness, or sorrow over the loss as many as six to ten years after the death. In fact, grief may never be completely finished. Many survivors periodically encounter its traces long years after the death.

The two tasks of grief have been described as emotional separation from the decedent and satisfying reconstruction of life apart from the decedent. The first task of separation is seldom accomplished significantly during grief's first year. By the end of the second year, however, most survivors have worked through the desire to hold on to, or get back, the decedent and are able to fully accept the reality of the death. This progress is marked by the survivor's willingness to see both the pleasant and unpleasant aspects of the lost relationship.

Although survivors begin rebuilding their lives early in bereavement, only after emotional detachment from the decedent is accomplished can the task of recovery from grief be earnestly pursued. The period of bereavement in which this task progresses is often called reinvolvement, attachment, adjustment, recovery, or reconstruction. It seems typically to take place between the second and fourth years following the death.

During recovery the survivor's pangs of grief come in waves, less frequent and less intense. Grief efforts focus predominantly on rebuilding a life in which the decedent is not an important living part. Survivors often move to a new locale, seek educational opportunities, start a new career, or enter new relationships during this time. Social ties are usually expanded, and hobbies or interests might be entertained with renewed zeal and satisfaction.

As recovery progresses, the survivor's sense of self is strengthened and self-esteem increases. A new self-confidence often develops if the survivor stretches the limits of perhaps previously untried skills and abilities. New attitudes towards life form.

Eventually, the survivor experiences hope that life without the decedent can be fulfilling and satisfying, that there is, afterall, a glowing life at the end of the tunnel of grief.

Full recovery from a significant loss is marked by absence of intense grief reactions, by achievement of emotional stability, by re-entry into socially satisfying relationships, by finding meaning and purpose in life, and by diminished need for outside or professional support. Recovery seems most likely between the ends of the second and fourth years of grieving, although some survivors continue to struggle toward it four to six years after the death.

Within three to four years of grieving, the majority of survivors are happily reengaged in life. They find life satisfying, and at least as rich and fulfilling as it was prior to the death. Many survivors even feel stronger and more competent than they did before the grief experience.

No matter how long recovery requires, survivors do not simply pass through their bereavement and leave it behind. Nor do they return fully to their former selves. They are not the individuals they were before the death. After surviving death and bereavement, survivors are at once somehow the same and somehow different. Though their lives can again be tasted, enjoyed, and savored in characteristic style, they will always experience a dash of loneliness, of sadness, and of yearning flavoring their lives.

Falling Short of Recovery

Recovery from grief, though always hoped for, is not always ensured. Grief can be stalled, retarded, aborted, obstructed, diverted, or interrupted before one or both of its tasks are completed. Some survivors do not successfully finish the grief work. Instead, they become casualties, or even fatalities of the process meant to help them suffer a death and emerge from bereavement alive.

Successful grieving results in the survivor's emancipation from emotional bondage to the decedent, readjustment to a life in which the decedent is missing, and formation of new relationships. When grief does not follow its expected course, these results are not achieved. In such cases, the survivor's experience may variously be called atypical grief, delayed grief, morbid grief, pathological grief,

107

or abnormal grief. These are all labels for essentially the same thing, that is, grief that has not ended in recovery.

What prevents some survivors from completing the grief work? Erich Lindemann [12] suggests that a survivor's attempt to avoid either the intense distress connected with grief or the expression of emotion necessary to exhaust it are common obstacles to successful grieving. The tendency to avoid the entire complex of grief reactions at any cost is indicated in various behaviors, like a survivor's refusing visits from others to avoid talking about the death.

Reactions that subvert grieving or that distort natural reactions Lindemann calls morbid or abnormal grief reactions. He suggests grief becomes abnormal, or nonfunctional, when such reactions are present. Grief reactions falling outside the realm of "normal" reactions generally arise because of delay or distortion of the normal grief reactions.

Delay of grieving is a particularly striking, and perhaps frequent, reaction to loss. Postponement of grief can have dire consequences for the survivor, as exemplified in experiences of individuals suffering delayed effects of trauma. Observations of combat war veterans experiencing symptoms of post-traumatic stress syndrome make increasingly evident the fact that delaying grief work can have enduring, disastrous, and catastrophic impact.

Grief may be put off, but it does not go away. Delayed grief continues to fester like a concealed psychic ulcer. The longer resolution of grief is delayed, the more insidious become the sores. Years after grief has normally run its course, survivors who have blocked its expression continue to use emotional energy to deal with unfinished grief reactions.

Abnormal grieving is also indicated by distorted reactions. Lindemann describes several common distortions that are signs of unresolved grief. Distorted grief reactions include:

1)   Patterns of overactivity in which the survivor acts as if a significant loss has not been experienced.

2)   Symptoms, illness, or behaviors once displayed by the decedent; development of any form of stress-related, psychosomatic illnesses.

3) Obvious changes in relationships with friends and relatives, like chronic irritability, avoidance of former social activities, progressive social isolation, expressed desire to be left alone, or disabling fear of antagonizing others; also, overflowing hostility that spreads throughout all relationships or is furiously targeted against specific people.

4) Concealment of anger and hostility at the expense of becoming wooden and formal; mask-like facial expression and an absence of emotional display.

5) Lasting loss of social interaction patterns indicated by inability to initiate any activity, restlessness or sleeplessness, lack of decisiveness, or loss of promise in anything other than routine, ordinary activities carried on with little enthusiasm.

6) Involvement in activities somehow detrimental to the survivor's social or economic welfare; loss of friends because of inappropriate behavior; self-punitive behavior, like alcohol or drug abuse, compulsive spending, or gambling, with no awareness of excessive guilt; inappropriate generosity, frivolous spending, or foolish financial dealings.

7) Agitated depression with elements of tension, insomnia, feelings of worthlessness, bitter self-accusation, or obvious desire for punishment.

Delays and distortions of reactions are normal among grieving survivors. Grief work starts and stops, bores full speed ahead and sluggishly plods along, is acknowledged and denied, indulged and avoided. Most survivors eventually accomplish the work, even if some take years longer than others.

However, when the delays or distortions are excessive, inadequate or incomplete resolution of grief is probable. Survivors who forestall grief work by delaying and distorting reactions suffer the saddest outcomes of survivorship. Stuck in their grief, blocking its necessary course, they hold on to elements of grief without awareness. They do not separate from the memory of the decedent or recover from the loss.

The number of survivors who do not successfully complete the grief work and remain troubled by the death years later may constitute a substantial minority. As many as one quarter (25%) of those experiencing grief are estimated to need some sort of professional assistance at one time or another during their bereavement. Therefore, grief counseling is commonly, and appropriately, sought by many survivors.

Some, but not the majority, of suicide survivors get "stuck" in their grief, blocked by reactions typical to suicide bereavement. Unresolved denial, shame, concealing the nature of the death, stigmatization, blame, and accusations or assumptions regarding responsibility for the death become obstructions to grief. These grief reactions are often at odds one with another and their expression can present the survivor a psychological dilemma.

Expression of one natural reaction sometimes conflicts with the expression of another equally natural reaction. For example, feeling anger toward the decedent is natural during grief, but its expression often increases the survivor's guilt. On the other hand, feeling guilt is also natural, yet its expression not only might block anger, it might also generate more anger. Essentially, then, the survivor is caught between contradictory emotional reactions, each an effective psychological expression of deeply experienced pain, yet at the same time, generating equally intolerable states of distress.

Suicide survivors are susceptible to finding themselves between this psychological "rock and hard place." More opportunities for psychological dilemmas result from the greater number of grief reactions natural to suicide bereavement. For example, greater intensity of guilt might seriously retard expression of anger. Excessive rage directed toward the decedent increases already troubling guilt. Similarly, searching for an acceptable explanation for the suicide conflicts with the need to separate, or detach, from the decedent, while the need to separate presses the survivor to get on with things before an acceptable answer has been discovered. The need for social contact can be blocked by shame or blame, and the cry for help might be muffled by avoidance of those who would respond to it.

Severe complications of grieving commonly result in incomplete or inadequate recovery and readjustment to life. Certainly, some suicide survivors do not fair well in grieving or recovery. These survivors often continue to deny the suicidal nature of the death many years later. They also fail to engage in comfortable social interactions for a long time after the death. Kjell Rudestam [22] believes suicide survivors who discover the decedent's body, who rationalize the suicide as a courageous or heroic act, who feel somehow stigmatized by the suicide, or who conceal the truth of the suicidal death from others are the ones most likely to find readjustment difficult after the death.

Complications in grieving and recovery after suicide result from the same basic obstructions encountered in other bereavements; not because the death was suicide, but because the survivor is unable to resolve grief reactions, to separate emotionally from the decedent, and to readjust to a life in which the decedent is missing. Manifestations of unresolved grief are the same among suicide survivors as those described by Lindemann regarding "normal" grief.

All survivors are susceptible to experiencing complications of grieving and difficulties in recovery. Such experiences are not unique to suicide bereavement. Additionally, grief complications and inadequate recovery are not universal among suicide survivors. In fact, the majority of suicide survivors show levels of recovery no different from any other survivor. Most need professional counseling no more during bereavement than others, they are just as likely to discover purpose and satisfaction in life after bereavement, to view their current lives as better than before in many ways, to establish financial and employment stability, and to become involved in new intimate and satisfying relationships.

Recovery appears especially likely after suicide when the relationship between the survivor and decedent was positive and minimally disruptive, when the survivor is successful in placing responsibility for cause of the suicide to factors outside of his control, and in some cases, when the decedent had somehow been a burden to the survivor prior to the death.

Though they may experience a greater number and intensity of grief reactions than others, suicide survivors do not require significantly more time to accomplish the grief work. Their recovery is usually well underway between the end of the second and fourth years following the death, and is firmly established no later than between the fourth and sixth years.

What Is So Different About Suicide Survivorship?

Death, regardless of cause, can be an excruciating and painful event in the survivor's life, bringing emotional, psychological, and physical upheaval. The grief that follows is nothing less than stressful and burdensome. For most survivors, the devastating intensity of bereavement will not be surpassed by any other event in their lives.

Since nearly all bereavements are traumatic in some ways, there seems little reason or utility in comparing the severity of one with another. While acknowledging this, it is safe to say, because so many grief reactions are common to suicide, that no bereavement could ever be more intense or severe than suicide bereavement.

Suicide bereavement is different. It is different because death by suicide is different. Suicide is more than death of a loved person. Additionally, it is death experienced suddenly and unexpectedly. It is death not by natural cause. Finally, it is death unquestionably deliberate, intentional, and self-inflicted.

As described in the previous four chapters, specific grief reactions result from each of these factors. Consequently, suicide bereavement is comprised of many grief reactions, including reactions common to all losses, reactions resulting from sudden and unexpected death, reactions resulting from other-than-natural death, and reactions largely unique to suicidal death. Suicide bereavement is different because it is comprised of such varied grief reactions, some of them seldom experienced by other survivors.

Grief reactions not experienced in "normal" bereavement are frequently described as exaggerations or distorted caricatures of "normal" grief features. They are called atypical, morbid, or abnormal grief reactions. Grief reactions following a suicide tend to be more intense, longer enduring, and of greater variety. They are beyond normal reactions which leads some people to consider suicide bereavement atypical, morbid, or abnormal. This is a grave misconception.

That two forms of bereavement have common elements does not necessarily nor logically mean one is derived from the other, atypical or not. Suicide bereavement is not "normal" bereavement gone haywire.

Suicide is death culturally considered abnormal. The belief a death is abnormal generally leads to the assumption reactions to it are also abnormal. However, suicide grief reactions are not abnormal derivatives of normal grief. They are natural reactions to a death that is different.

Suicide survivorship is comprised, in part, of intense "normal" reactions to a significant loss and, in part, of special reactions derived from the sudden, other-than-natural, and self-inflicted nature of the death. The suicide grief process is a complex interaction of all these reactions. It is a "normal" or natural consequence to a form of death socially judged abnormal.

Let's emphasize that the experience of special grief reactions common in suicide grief does not mean this bereavement is complicated, atypical, morbid, or abnormal. Bereavement after suicide is not, in any sense, abnormal. The reactions described in previous chapters are natural reactions to the special features of suicidal death. Suicide bereavement is different than other bereavements, but natural all the same.

Ultimately, comparing grief experiences of suicide survivors with those of others may be unproductive. Although suicide bereavement is primarily a normal response to significant loss, it is also something more. Suicide bereavement is different from other bereavements, with good reason. Some elements of suicidal death are unique. Some elements of societal reactions to the death are unique. Finally, some elements of the suicide grief process are unique.

The combination of these unique elements almost demands the final outcome of bereavement will be different for the suicide survivor. The death and its processing are different. So too, then, should be its resolution.

Fortunately, and encouragingly, for suicide survivors, the differences inherent in suicide bereavement do not mean survivors suffer atypical or abnormal recovery from grief. On the contrary, most suicide survivors do as well in long-term recovery as do other survivors.

Grief's Combat Veterans

To understand suicide bereavement better, it might be helpful to relate it to another familiar experience in our society, that is, to the experience of war's combat veterans.

Stresses, tragedies, and hardships exist for all people in the military during war periods. Commonalities of experience are based upon being anywhere in the service during a war. While these similar features comprise a large part of wartime experience, the reactions to the war, the resolution of psychological conflicts resulting from it, and the aftermath when it ends are qualitatively and quantitatively different for veterans who engaged the enemy first hand in combat compared with veterans who served in the rear areas of the combat theater or those who remained stateside.

More succinctly, there are important differences between war experiences of combat veterans and those of noncombatant veterans. The differences make it impossible for noncombatants to fully appreciate, comprehend, or identify with the experience of combatants. Their experiences just are not the same.

It is clear that war's combat veterans, after facing uncertain death and inflicting harm upon others, encounter difficulties in readjusting to peace that other veterans do not. A minor percentage of returning combat veterans fails at this readjustment and become post facto casualties, even fatalities, of the war experience. Some rear echelon and stateside veterans also fail to successfully readjust to peacetime life, so this experience is not unique to the minority of combat veterans. Most veterans, however, including combat veterans, make these adjustments and reenter civilian life adequately.

It is also important to note severe complications and difficulties in readjustment are not universal among all combat veterans. Their war experience might be more intense, stressful, and traumatic than other veterans, but the majority of combat veterans do not encounter overwhelming obstacles in their recovery from the war or in their readjustment to peace. The combat veterans will, however, be forever different because of their experiences.

Post-traumatic stress syndrome among Vietnam's combat veterans has been sensationalized in the media. However, research has shown that the vast majority of America's combat veterans from Vietnam were able to adjust adequately in the aftermath of their traumatic war experiences. Most of them have gone on to make productive, purposeful, and satisfying lives for themselves.

Comparison of the relationship of suicide survivorship to other bereavements can be made to the relationship between combat experiences and noncombat experiences. The grief process is war. Survivors are the veterans. Suicide survivors are the combat veterans. Survivors of unexpected and other-than-natural death besides suicide are the rear area noncombatants. The survivors of expected natural death are the stateside noncombatants.

While similar features are found in the experiences of all survivors and all veterans, special and significant differences exist among suicide survivors and combatants. In no way does this suggest bereavements resulting from nonsuicidal death are not traumatic experiences. Death is a tragic event for all concerned. The resultant grief process, like war, is stressful for all who live through it. For suicide survivors, like combatants, the experience is different.

Just as it is true that a few survivors of other bereavements do not successfully finish their grieving, it is also true that a majority of suicide survivors do find hope, purpose, and reward in the completion of their grief work.

The analogy drawn between suicide survivors and combat veterans is meant to emphasize a point often missed by those who do not understand bereavement following suicide. As individuals engaged in the serious business of suicide bereavement, suicide survivors forever leave behind cherished parts of themselves; parts like innocence, simple trust, naivety, spontaneity, a view of the world as a safe place, and the freedom to love easily. They emerge from their experience transformed, possessing different views and attitudes toward life than they had before the suicide. They, the combatants, experience an event and a grief process other survivors cannot fully appreciate or comprehend. Their transformation in the war zone of suicide bereavement makes them forever different.

Although made different by their experiences, suicide survivors do get on with their lives. They *do* recover admirably, finding meaning and satisfaction in lives forever changed.

CHAPTER TEN
Surviving Suicide Bereavement

"No suicide dies alone. His exodus from life hurts everyone around him."

William L. Coleman [34]

Grieving is an extremely disruptive experience in a person's life regardless of cause of death. Physical, emotional, and psychological stresses are amplified. Behaviors and habit patterns are disturbed. Relationships with others are strained and often severed. The risks of illness, accidents, and death are increased. In sum, grief can be a dangerous and possibly life-threatening experience.

How do people survive grieving and get on with their lives? Survivors take any of several avenues for getting through their grief. Some count on the support of family and friends. Others do it alone, isolating themselves and keeping their grief private. Many survivors seek professional help to deal with grief.

Certainly individuals grieve in their own unique ways. Those who do rebuild their lives credit various factors important in their recoveries. One factor, in particular, is mentioned consistently in the stories of survivors who master grief. It is the opportunity to talk openly, freely, and often at great length about their grief.

Talking about grieving is important, probably essential, to the resolution of grief. When asked to look back upon the years of their bereavement, many survivors wonder if some early counseling would have made their grieving more bearable. Even those who were surrounded by supportive friends and family believed an objective perspective from someone with an understanding of grief would have eased some of the more troubling aspects of bereavement. It is these troubling features that survivors often find themselves trying to figure out alone.

People are frequently at a loss when it comes to consoling, comforting, supporting, or nurturing the survivor. Many survivors find themselves at times without anyone who understands the troubling reactions they face. For this reason, it is common for survivors to seek the professional help of a minister, doctor, counselor, psychologist, or psychiatrist.

Cause of death does not seem to affect the decision to try counseling. Among adult survivors as many as 75% might try professional counseling at least once after the death. Nearly 65% will return for counseling more than once.

Although suicide survivors face a complex array of grief reactions like those described in earlier chapters, they are able to successfully recover from grief as well as other survivors. Additionally, they appear to accomplish their grieving in much the same manner as others and do so in similar periods of time.

How Suicide Survivors Grieve

Suicide survivors work through grief in familiar ways. Many are fortunate enough to have understanding and supportive family and friends in whom they confide. Some grieve alone, dealing with the many grief reactions as best they can and managing, with time, to put their lives back together. Suicide survivors engage in professional counseling in numbers similar to other survivors. In fact, 65% of adult suicide survivors seek counseling at least once, and 64% return for counseling more than once.

As in other bereavements, a few suicide survivors come to terms with the nature of the death, accept the death, and re-engage in a satisfying life relatively quickly. This occurs within the first year following the death in some cases. Most suicide survivors work more slowly than this through the grief process, moving gradually, resolutely, and often deliberately toward the resolution of their grief. Among these survivors, separation from intense attachment to the deceased has usually been accomplished well before the fourth year. Also, by the end of the fourth year, reinvolvement in life has typically progressed to the point the survivor believes life has meaning, is worth living, is satisfying, and is better in some ways than before the death.

Finally, just like in other bereavements, a few suicide survivors continue to struggle with their grief as long as six years after the death. Life continues to be terribly disrupted and painful for these survivors. Time does not bring healing. For these survivors, professional help may be a necessary catalyst for resolving personal and grief issues.

Help With The Healing

Suicide survivors are a special group of people, made so by the various aspects of suicide bereavement. Relationships between professionals and suicide survivors also have special aspects. Edwin Shneidman [35] coined the term postvention for special efforts directed toward suicide survivors.

The goal of postvention is to help suicide survivors deal with emotional and psychological reactions to the death. Shneidman [10] describes postvention as activities that reduce after-effects of a traumatic event. These activities help survivors live longer, more productive, and less stressful lives than they might do otherwise.

Professionals recommend that postvention efforts should begin as soon after the death as possible, particularly within the first 24 to 72 hours. Such efforts are important not only in the initial period of shock following the suicide, but also in the more enduring day-to-day living with grief that continues beyond the first year of bereavement.

Shneidman maintains that postvention adds a measure of stability in the survivor's life, providing interpersonal relationships in which honest feelings need not be suppressed or dissembled. Ideally, postvention provides the survivor an arena to express normally guarded emotions that might not otherwise be aired. The survivor freely vents "negative" emotions like anger, guilt, envy, shame, and irritation. Shneidman adds that most survivors are willing or eager to talk with others about their grief, especially to professionally-oriented persons.

Contact must be established between survivor and professional for postvention efforts to be undertaken. However, survivors seldom initiate this contact early in bereavement. Considering the overwhelming complex of reactions occurring early in grief, it is not surprising a rational decision to seek professional help is beyond the emotional and psychological inclinations of most survivors. Additionally, Lee Ann Hoff [36] believes another reason suicide survivors get such little early help is that most suicides do not occur among people who have received prior counseling help and, therefore, the survivors are not likely to consider it for themselves early in their grief.

If suicide survivors are little inclined to seek professional help early when it would be most advantageous, how are postvention efforts to be initiated? Edwin Shneidman, Lee Ann Hoff and others maintain that an active out-reach program for suicide survivors is an ideal and basic component of any comprehensive community crisis service.

Many Crisis Centers and Suicide Prevention Centers have developed postventive out-reach programs. Donna Junghardt [37] describes such a suicide survivor follow-up program established by the San Bernadino County Department of Public Health in California for the purpose of bringing support and comfort to family survivors. The out-reach program establishes contact with survivors 24 to 48 hours after the death and before the funeral, when possible. This particular postvention program proceeds through three phases.

Phase one begins with the initial contact of the survivor. The goals of this phase are to help the survivor withstand the initial shock of immense loss and to increase his or her understanding of basic grief emotions. Facing the reality and facts about the suicide are not critical during this initial phase.

Phase two takes place during the six months after the funeral. Regular meeting times are set up with either individual family members or with a group. In the first week after the funeral two or three meetings are sometimes necessary. Afterwards, weekly meetings are typically adequate for about three or four weeks. The initial crisis period is usually passed after the sixth week, and meetings are then scheduled at two or three week intervals. The goals of these meetings are to facilitate reintegration of the family, to help the survivor deal with the grief process, to help him understand the dynamics of grieving, and to deal with whatever emotions, social problems, or crises arise.

Phase three begins after the six month anniversary of the suicide. At this point renewal and rejuvenation begin to take place and little need for professional contact exists. The survivors are revisited around the suicide's first year anniversary to see how well the family is doing and to determine if any problems have developed that might require more therapeutic contact.

The out-reach concept is effective for suicide survivors because, as suggested above, so few survivors perceive a need to contact a professional during the early period of emotional and psychological shock following the death. Few survivors look for this contact during the first year of bereavement when it would be most helpful, although many survivors say they would have welcomed the offer of help from a trained professional at the time of the suicide.

Out-reach programs are effective, but they are difficult to conduct, primarily because suicide survivors are hard to identify from among other survivors. Cause of death in the case of suicide is no longer reported in obituaries. Also, confidentiality issues restrict access to death certificates and prohibit dissemination of information by funeral directors. Therefore, out-reach personnel must find other ways to engage contact with the survivors, usually by media advertising of available services.

The root of such issues remains negative social beliefs and attitudes that darkly color suicide. As long as suicide is shrouded in stigma, myth, and taboo, out-reach programs offering service to its survivors will be deterred from establishing life-giving contacts. Responsibility to initiate postvention efforts, then, will continue to rest with individuals least able to do so; that is, the suicide survivors themselves.

Where do suicide survivors turn for help in grieving? Quite frequently, instead of individual counseling, suicide survivors try finding support in one group or another. Most adult survivors are aware of several types of support groups available in their communities. Among these are included; survivors' groups (e.g., Theos for spouses & Compassionate Friends for parents), single parent groups, singles groups, and special groups like Alanon.

Typically, these groups are open-ended, meaning the participants change from meeting to meeting. Also, they usually do not follow goal-oriented formats. As helpful as support groups might be, they are not likely to meet the special needs of survivors early in bereavement.

Suicide survivors who try a support group often do not go back after only one or two meetings, especially if the group was not specifically structured to deal with the special grief reactions following suicide. Some survivors, searching for a source of help, understanding, and encouragement, repeat this pattern in more than one support group.

Abandoning support groups is common among survivors in their first year of bereavement. Survivors waiting until after the second year, when grief has diminished and recovery is underway to some degree, benefit more from these same support groups. We might conclude from this that support groups not directly focused upon the grief of suicide survivors provide help in recovery but not in dealing with severe grief reactions. In other words, open-ended and general support groups do not adequately help the survivor resolve the many intense reactions and deeply painful experiences that are part and parcel of suicide survivorship.

Both Allen Battle [38] and Adina Wrobleski [39] recognize the difficulty suicide survivors encounter within support groups and recommend that they turn to groups that address unique features of suicide bereavement. In recent years suicide survivors' groups have been organized in many communities around the country. The American Association of Suicidology's directory provides a listing of 197 such support groups established in 42 of the states and 11 in the provinces of Canada (see Pg. 127).

What Are Suicide Survivors' Support Groups Like?

Many suicide survivors' groups use an open structure in which membership is not fixed from one meeting to next, no agenda or predetermined topics are covered, and no limit is placed on the number of meetings. Size of these groups is usually not set, but rather is determined simply by the number of survivors who happen to attend any particular meeting. As few as five or six people might be present at one meeting and as many as 15 to 20 at another.

Other survivors' groups follow grief-therapy formats in which the same survivors attend from start to completion, a structured format with specific goals is imposed upon the meetings, and a limit is established for the number of group meetings to be conducted. These groups usually include between six to twelve survivors.

The difference in formats is an important consideration. Individuals attending suicide survivors' groups can be anywhere between a few weeks to 15 years or more beyond the suicide. Obviously, survivors in the early period of grief have different needs than those well past this stage, and one particular support group usually does not meet the needs of both.

How survivors respond to a group largely depends on its structure and composition. Suicide survivors commonly find little satisfaction in open and nonstructured suicide support groups when they are in the initial year of bereavement. They abandon these groups as frequently as they abandon the more general support groups mentioned above. Adina Wrobleski reports a 40% dropout rate among Suicide Survivor Support Groups established in Minneapolis, MN. The dropouts went to one or two meetings and did not return afterwards. These suicide survivors who give up on support groups may be individuals still in the most painful stages of grieving.

Survivors early in their grief are best served by a group providing both structure and information focusing upon special features of suicide bereavement. Suicide grief-therapy groups more frequently follow this format than do open suicide support groups.

The primary goals of grief-therapy are to facilitate the survivor's separation from the decedent and to promote healthy recovery from grief. To these ends, grief-therapy groups use structured formats dealing directly with grief experiences. Meetings are scheduled regularly over a period of several months to help survivors get through the trying stage of bereavement. Usually, 10 to 15 meetings, lasting 1 1/2 hours and held every two weeks are sufficient in meeting the therapeutic goals.

Grief-therapy groups have shown encouraging results with suicide survivors. Allen Battle reports most survivors participating in the Memphis, TN "Survivor of Suicide" therapy groups believe their needs were met in less than ten meetings. Some survivors were helped by remaining through 10 to 15 meetings. Only a few felt they had not been helped by being in such a group.

An example of a structured grief-therapy group for suicide survivors was conducted at the Moorhead State University Counseling Center in Moorhead, MN. The group augmented an existing open suicide survivors' group in Fargo, North Dakota. Its goals were to provide insight into the experience of suicide bereavement, to foster an understanding and acceptance of the suicidal death, to provide an arena in which survivors could openly acknowledge and express grief reactions commonly most troubling after a suicide, and to facilitate uncomplicated resolution of the bereavement.

The grief-therapy group met for ten 1 1/2 hour sessions, one evening every two weeks. Up to twelve adult members who were parents, children, siblings, or friends of someone who had completed suicide attended the meetings. The group was formed to assist survivors who were anywhere within the first two years of bereavement, but did include survivors a little beyond that period, also.

The ten meeting itinerary included the following agenda:

Meeting One: Is my grief different because the death was self-inflicted?
Meeting Two: Why did he/she do it?
Meeting Three: Could I have prevented the death?
Meeting Four: Dealing with rejection.
Meeting Five: Dealing with guilt.
Meeting Six: Dealing with anger and shame.
Meeting Seven: The wonderful life before the death.
Meeting Eight: The awful life before the death.
Meeting Nine: Can my life be better again?
Meeting Ten: How do I finish this grief?

The members evaluated the ten meetings by rating each on a scale of one through ten, running from "not productive at all" (1), "not very helpful" (3), "somewhat helpful" (5), "helpful" (7), to "very helpful" (10). The meetings were all predominantly scored with ratings between seven and ten. Only 5% of the ratings fell below the helpful range.

Regardless of structure and composition, effective suicide survivors' support groups focus on concerns related to the suicidal nature of the death. Issues and concerns especially important to suicide survivors include:

* Searching for the meaning of the death or for an explanation of the suicide.

* Mental images of the suicidal death.

* Dealing with negative social views and reactions toward suicide and the survivor.

* Learning to talk about the death and decedent in an honest, nondefensive way.

* Resolving feelings of anger, depression, shame, blame, and guilt.

* Experiencing seemingly crazy, frightening, and confusing thoughts, feelings, or behaviors.

* Doubts regarding the "normalcy" of bereavement.

* Matters of faith and religion.

* The devastating loss of self-esteem.

* Breaking through the survivor's preoccupation with the suicidal nature of the death and getting on with bereavement.

* Repairing the survivor's life and family.

Suicide survivors experience special benefits within suicide survivor groups. For example, Bruce Danto [40] reports that members of a suicide survivors'group therapy program in the Detroit, Michigan area, quickly formed deep and meaningful relationships.

Among other benefits suicide survivors commonly experience within such groups are:

* Relief in sharing their stories with others able to identify compassionately with their grief.

* Increased understanding of the dynamics of suicide.

* Assistance in accepting the reality of the suicidal death.

* Support in working through the grief crisis and in dealing with stresses of daily living in the aftermath of the death.

* Opportunities to express feelings, including negative ones toward the deceased, in a supportive, non-threatening, and non-rejecting atmosphere.

* Encouragement to talk about, or hear about, the suicide over and over.

* Support and encouragement in helping children.

This last factor is a tremendous benefit of participating in a suicide survivor support group. As Lee Ann Hoff notes, parents may need special help in explaining a suicide to children. There is an almost universal wish to hide details of a suicide from children,

125

usually arising from a mistaken belief doing so spares them unnecessary pain.

Hoff maintains parents often do not comprehend the serious results that are possible from trying to hide facts from children. She reminds us that children usually know more than they are given credit for and, in the least, know that something much more terrible than an accident has taken place. Hoff insists that suicide is best explained clearly, simply, and in a manner consistent with a child's level of development and understanding. It is also important to encourage children to ask questions and express feelings.

Where To Find Suicide Survivors' Support Groups

This chapter suggests that nearly three quarters of all survivors have grief concerns serious enough that they will try professional counseling at least once during their bereavement. Survivors do not usually avail themselves of such support early in the grief process when it would be most helpful for them to do so. Unfortunately, because suicide survivors are difficult to identify through obituary articles, postvention efforts directed at supporting them through the initial period of their grief are often not implemented.

At least a year passes after the death before many survivors look for professional help. In some cases, the motivation for doing so derives from the fact that, in a year's time, the effects of grieving accumulate and the survivor uses up all the personal resources available. In other cases, the survivor is simply unprepared for the duration of grief and becomes concerned something is wrong. In either case, a great number of survivors enlist the counseling support of some professional before the end of the second year. Additionally, many survivors attempt to ease the stresses of grieving by participating in some sort of support group.

Since it is often the suicide survivors, themselves, who must initiate postvention efforts, it would be helpful for them to know where to look for assistance. Suicide Prevention and Crisis Centers are usually appropriate places to inquire about the availability of services for survivors. It would also be beneficial if those providing special services to suicide survivors advertised widely through various media.

Two sources giving updated information about available suicide survivor groups in the United States and Canada are:

1) Survivors of Suicide Support Groups in the US & Canada

   Published by: American Association of Suicidology
   2459 S. Ash Street
   Denver, CO 80222
   (303) 692-0985

2) Directory of Survivors of Suicide Support Groups
   in the US & Canada

   Published by: Survivors of Suicide
   Suicide Prevention Center, Inc.
   184 Salem Avenue
   Dayton, OH 45406
   (513) 223-9096

Attending a suicide survivors support group is recommended for all survivors, regardless of their relationship to the deceased. This is especially true for survivors in the first year of their bereavement. Survivors should understand that their first few meetings may give rise to increased emotionality as feelings surface and that a decision not to go back to the group is common. However, the benefit of attending a support group increases if the survivor goes to at least six meetings. Most survivors find that the initial discomfort of dealing with grief within a group decreases as familiarity with the group experience develops. A useful rule of thumb is:

"Attend six meetings, then decide if the group is helpful."

CHAPTER ELEVEN
Further conclusions

"A suicide is never completely forgotten or forgiven."

Pamela Cantor [31]

Patterns of recovery

Suggestions that suicide survivors experience more frequent and severe grief reactions have, in the past, led to the conclusion that these survivors are inevitably doomed to complicated bereavements and troubled readjustments to life. This conclusion was simply not true. The belief that suicide shackles and torments its survivors more than other forms of death is largely a myth.

Although suicide bereavement often includes many special grief reactions, and its onslaught can nearly be overwhelming, the outcome for survivors is more promising than might be expected. In fact, the outcome of suicide bereavement is similar to that of any other bereavement.

The majority of suicide survivors, grieve and recover adequately and satisfactorily. These survivors eventually reestablish themselves in a life that holds meaning, purpose, satisfactions, and day-to-day concerns no longer directly tied to the experience of grief. Of course, some suicide survivors do not fair well in their grieving and recovery. For them, the suicide and its consequent grief is a devastating experience that impacts upon the rest of their lives. These survivors, victims of suicide, are in the unfortunate minority.

That the majority of adult survivors do well in the aftermath of suicide is surprising, considering the grief they must negotiate. This does not imply that suicide survivors are not scarred by the death. Certainly they are. It would be more accurate to say, however, that they and their lives are changed by the suicide, not destroyed by it.

Memories of the circumstances surrounding the suicide are likely to be imprinted vividly on the survivor's mind and remain so ten, fifteen, twenty years after the death. The suicidal event itself may never be forgotten. Many survivors continue to ask "why?" years after the suicide and never completely resolve the search for explanation of the death. They also long regret the death, on some level, and fantasize how different life would be had it not happened.

Enduring reactions like these long retain the emotional power to touch off sorrow. Yet, such lingering traces of grief do not tie suicide survivors endlessly to their bereavement. Like other survivors, most suicide survivors recover the capacity to find meaning, satisfaction, and enjoyment in life following their grief.

The ways by which suicide survivors accomplish their recoveries and readjustments are similar to those of other survivors. They often credit the resolution of grief to the availability of understanding friends or family, a deeply felt responsibility toward children still at home, a strong spiritual or religious faith, a life stable in all other aspects, a practical attitude toward death developed early in life (e.g., "We all have to die sometime. Those left behind have to make the most of things."), and/or just doing their best while giving grief free rein to run its course.

Talking through emotional grief reactions openly and honestly is crucial to successful bereavement. Denial or concealment of any aspect of the experience inhibits the grief process. It is particularly important that suicide survivors talk about the suicide and what it means to them. Survivors who recover satisfactorily are those able to confront the nature of the death and honestly deal with it.

Apparently, the opportunity to talk with anyone concerned enough to listen about the suicide and the grief reactions that follow it helps the survivor manage the grief. It does not seem to matter whether suicide survivors talk with friends, family members, ministers, or professional counselors; among those who frequently talk about the death openly with others, satisfactory recovery and readjustment are the rule rather than the exception.

Survivors least likely to recover adequately from their grief seem to be those who either are isolated from understanding and supportive social contact or are unable to bring themselves to discuss the suicide. If a survivor does not talk honestly about the death, partially unfinished, repressed, or unresolved grief is a common result.

One universal consequence of inadequately completed grief apparently is that future grieving revitalizes buried grief, like reopening a festering wound. Survivors with unfinished grief suffer later emotional recollection of prior deaths whenever they experience new bereavements. Sometimes these survivors have to work through old grief in order to make sense of new grief.

It seems most survivors reexperience old grief during new bereavements, if in no other form than memories believed long forgotten. In fact, it may be that all grief we experience in our lifetime is unconsciously linked by a hidden emotional thread.

How troublesome later resurrection of old grief becomes depends on how well grief was resolved in the first place. If the earlier bereavement was curtailed or incomplete, a survivor may have to expend a great deal of energy either to complete the old grief or to keep it buried beneath psychological defenses weakened by current grief. Ultimately, the consequence of unfinished, repressed, or unresolved grief is that new bereavements can be all the more crippling when fueled by old grief.

The Intent To Die

To better understand a suicide survivor's grief experience it is important we recognize that part of this experience is determined by social perceptions of self-inflicted death. As explained in Chapter Four, current cultural attitudes and conventions divide death into normal and suicidal, depending on the apparent cause of death.

It helps to recognize that following non-suicidal death, grief navigates a course that is partly dictated by the social belief that such death is normal. Following a suicide, grief is significantly influenced by the social belief that suicide is abnormal. As if swift, unexpected grief is not traumatic enough, suicide survivors suffer reactions resulting from the perceived inappropriateness of self-inflicted death.

Only after a suicide does the label attached to the death so intensely affect the survivor. Suicide survivors would not experience many of the additional grief reactions inherent only in self-inflicted death if suicidal death was not viewed as abnormal, that is, if it was accepted as a normal form of death.

The division of death into normal or suicidal (abnormal) potentially results in special grief experiences, and sometimes devastating consequences, for the suicide survivor. This result is unfortunate because separation of death into normal and suicidal is based on a false inference by our society.

The common thread presumed to tie all so-called normal deaths is the absence of intention or wish to die on the part of the decedent. That deaths considered normal have this feature in common is a social illusion.

We can never be completely certain whether there is intent or wish to die in any death. This is true in death by natural cause, accident, homicide, and suicide. There seem to be cases in which a person with a desire to die did so by means not obviously suicidal. Some people with terminal illness die before their prognosis would suggest they should. Many people die in car accidents that appear completely avoidable. Some homicide victims appear to have deliberately provoked fatal attacks.

Deaths in which intent to die is absent but appears to be present are also common. Many deaths look like suicides, but might just as well be accidents or homicides.

Interestingly, then, grief is not entirely a reaction to the reality of the death itself. It is also partly a reaction to the label given to the death by social convention. Therefore, even though a person dies intentionally (whether by conscious or unconscious motive), and his intention is not obvious, the death will be labeled something other than suicide. Such deaths are considered normal and the survivor experiences a "normal" bereavement. On the other hand, if a death is an accident, yet is labeled a suicide, the survivor experiences suicide bereavement, not accidental death bereavement.

It is impossible to know if the decedent intended to die, regardless of the label attached to the death. Once the label of suicide is applied, however, the conclusion is drawn that the death was not "inevitable" at that time. This assumption is based on the belief that, had it not been for the suicide, the decedent would have been blessed with a much longer life.

This belief does not acknowledge any chance that the decedent's life might have ended just as abruptly by terminal illness, natural disaster, random homicide, or accident. It also may serve, on a deeper psychological level, as a defense against facing the realities of human death. More specifically, the strong reaction to this form of "premature" death may serve to unconsciously protect us from our own fear of dying.

We mortals have not learned to face and accept death. We are not comfortable with, nor do we like to acknowledge, the fact that death for any of us can be just an instant away. Part of our troubled reaction to suicide, then, may be that it makes us confront death sooner than we feel necessary. Suicide disturbs us because it forces us to face issues surrounding death before such confrontation is "inevitable."

The Imprint Of Inevitability

Our society considers suicide an abnormal behavior, partly because it brings about a death sooner than is acceptable. That a suicidal death was not "inevitable" is not the only thing that makes it abnormal, however. If inevitability were the only factor, homicides and accidents, neither necessarily inevitable, might also be considered abnormal. This is not the case. Accidents and homicides are not viewed socially as abnormal. Suicide, on the other hand, is seldom accepted as normal or inevitable under any circumstances.

It is the combination of the intention to die and the apparent senseless nature of the death that leads us to view suicide as abnormal. Consequently, because suicidal death is perceived as neither "normal" nor as carrying the "imprint of inevitability", an absolute mandate for its prevention has been generated. Is there any other form of death with such a weighty mandate?

Preventing suicide

The demand to prevent suicide has social, legal, and moral roots. When a suicide occurs, the mandate for its prevention weighs heavily upon the survivors with powerful social, legal, and moral implications. The survivors bear the brunt when the mandate for preventing suicide fails.

Society often seems psychologically and emotionally blind to the fact that preventing suicide is a difficult endeavor at best, but also is, in an important way, an act that forestalls eventual death. And, must we prolong life regardless of the consequences or the quality of the life preserved?

Most professionals working in the field of suicide prevention react strongly to questions of this nature. Rightly so. In most cases, it is a compassionate and human endeavor to prevent someone's death. Life-saving efforts are especially humane when the quality of the person's life is somehow enhanced and improved after the prevention.

A person's life is not always made better by its saving. In some cases, preventing a person from ending his or her life is nothing short of a sentence to live out a hopeless, painful, and humiliating life; a life devoid of anything that might be considered humanly satisfying. The compassion and humanity in interfering with an individual's choice of putting an end to such pain, regardless of how distasteful this alternative is to us, is a sensitive topic and open to debate. Acknowledging such opinions, in July and September, 1989, the Michigan and Georgia courts ruled in favor of allowing paralyzed adults to make their own right-to-die decisions (Time Magazine, September 18, 1989, pg 67).

Suicide: a normal death?

Our society is hesitant, perhaps frightened, to accept the premise that, if death is normal, so too must be death by suicide. Perhaps we are afraid that accepting suicide as a normal death might somehow be an endorsement of suicidal acts. This need not be the case.

It is not a matter of advocating or even condoning suicide. We will never like self-inflicted death, regardless of the circumstances of the decedent's life. The question posed here is, can we stop viewing suicide as a sin, a weakness of character, an act of insanity, an extreme expression of inherent selfishness, a symptom of family discord, or as a failure of others to respond in a caring and timely way. Can we instead accept suicide as a normal means of death? Can we accept suicide as a normal reaction to chronic and severe depression, a normal behavioral response to a yet undiscovered neuro-chemical disturbance or biological imbalance, a normal consequence of a life sadly rife with incomprehensible pain, suffering, and hopelessness, or as an unfortunate, but normal, consequence of an ill-considered impulse which temporarily steals away a person's ability to think and behave rationally? Difficult questions, yes.

It was not the objective of this book to argue the right or wrong of self-inflicted death. The hope expressed here is that suicide survivors will be freed from the adverse grief reactions engendered by society's views of death by suicide. Obviously, our social views have had little affect in preventing suicide. Nor do our conventions have any impact upon the decedent once the act has been completed.

Our social views and attitudes do, however, carry serious implications and consequences for the suicide survivor, the innocent victim of self-inflicted death. Acceptance of suicide as a "normal" form of death might well diminish the special experiences of suicide survivors.

Suicide survivors are likely to continue grieving in the manner described in this book. They are likely to continue to do so for as long as social illusion stigmatizes suicidal death as somehow very different than other forms of death. Yet, suicide survivors' bereavements are normal, dictated in part by a significant personal loss, by an unexpected and other-than-natural death, and, finally, by a death socially viewed as abnormal.

Grief reactions resulting from the significant loss and from the unexpected and other-than-natural features of suicide are not likely to change. However, suicide survivors need not be damned to experience such unique grief reactions like denial of the cause of death, embarrassment regarding the death, fear of insanity, moral concerns, or communication problems. Social beliefs and attitudes can change. Myths can be assailed. If such changes are fostered regarding the experience of suicide in our society, the grief experience of its survivors might hopefully be relieved of the additional reactions resulting from the socially-viewed inappropriateness of the death.

The survivors' entitlement

May we all, survivors, family members, friends, and professional helpers alike, strive tirelessly and boldly to provide suicide survivors the dignity to which the experience of bereavement entitles them.

APPENDIX A
ASSESSING SUICIDE GRIEF: THE GRIEF EXPERIENCE QUESTIONNAIRE

"Survivors are saddled with an unhealthy complex of emotions: shame, guilt, anger, perplexity. They are obsessed with the death."

Edwin Shneidman [25]

We are not well prepared for experiencing death--our own or someone's close to us. We tend to avoid thoughts of death until it slams into our lives, and the choice of hiding from it becomes impossible. That survivors who have not been through a bereavement are surprised by the turmoil grief brings to their lives is understandable.

Grief's intensity, severity, and duration can turn *anyone* "frantic with panic." Suicide bereavement has even greater potential for creating confusion among survivors, even among those who have experienced previous deaths and prior griefs. Veteran survivors have said that grieving earlier deaths did not prepare them for what happens after a suicide.

Survivors often wonder during bereavement if something is wrong with them. Questions they ask reflect their confusion. "What's going on with me?" "Is this normal?" "Do other people feel this way?" "How am I doing compared to other people who've had this happen?" "Can things get worse than this?" "Will things get any better?" "Am I over it?" "Will I ever really be myself again?" "When will this grief be over?"

Most survivors welcome information about how well they are managing their grief. Since they are typically unable to objectively define or assess their own bereavements, such information must be provided by others. Support groups frequently are a productive source for this information, as are professional counselors. As suggested in Chapter Ten, seeking sensitive and understanding support from others during bereavement is a positive step toward managing grief's onslaught.

Assurance that personal reactions to death are "normal" gives suicide survivors some relief in the face of troubling emotions. Not all survivors attend groups or seek professional help. For suicide survivors who choose not to participate in group therapies or in counseling, the following questionnaire may prove useful.

Measuring A Survivor's Grief

The Grief Experience Questionnaire (GEQ) is a measurement of grief reactions. It has had limited use in a number of research projects among suicide survivors and in clinical settings as an assessment tool (Barrett & Scott, 1989 [41]). The content of the questionnaire can help define the suicide grief experience and measure its progress.

The GEQ is comprised of fifty-five questions, measuring the content and intensity of grief reactions. The questions are based on common reactions as experienced among all bereaved people, among unexpected death survivors, and among only suicide survivors.

The previous chapters described many grief reactions common after suicide. The GEQ does not measure each of these nor does it include all grief reactions possible during bereavement. The GEQ's design assumes the presence of many grief reactions to some degree. Therefore, the GEQ excludes some generally common grief reactions and measures only a sample of significant reactions.

All 55 GEQ questions represent "normal" grief reactions after a suicide. The specific concerns measured include: the survivor's general physical condition, the search for an acceptable explanation for the suicide, levels of social isolation and loss of support, the feeling suicide negatively and permanently marks the survivor as different from other survivors, sense of guilt, sharing of complicity and responsibility for the suicide, levels of embarrassment over the cause, nature, or circumstances surrounding the death, feeling of deliberate abandonment and rejection by the deceased, and involvement in self-destructive or life-threatening behaviors on the survivor's part.

The GEQ can be usefully completed any time during bereavement. Answering the questions within the first year -- optimally, six months after the suicide -- provides a basis for determining how the survivor is managing grief. The GEQ also provides useful information when completed more than once, for example, every six months throughout the four years following the death.

GEQ responses can provide a survivor with a concrete record of some of his or her experiences following the suicide. If the survivor is inclined to seek support from a group or a professional helper, these responses can be helpful in focusing attention on important areas of grief. Survivors interested in a more comprehensive assessment of grief may want to follow the instructions provided in Appendix B.

The Grief Experience Questionnaire

The full 55 item GEQ is presented in the next pages. An answer sheet and instructions for obtaining a detailed assessment of a GEQ are provided at the bottom of the answer sheet in Appendix B. The average time to complete the questionnaire is less than 20 minutes.

The first time the GEQ is completed, consider whether each reaction has been experienced in the period since the suicide happened. Circle the response indicating how frequently the reaction was encountered. If more than two years have passed since the death, consider whether or not you have experienced the reactions only in the previous two years.

If the GEQ is completed a second time, consider only the period between completions in responding to the questions. In other words, subsequent completions disregard the months covered by previous GEQs, thereby tracking the grief since the GEQ was last completed. Later GEQ completions provide information about the progress of grief.

GRIEF EXPERIENCE QUESTIONNAIRE

In completing each item, consider the experiences you have had since the death (or since the last time you completed the GEQ). You may find that some of the questions do not apply to you. For these, you circle "never." For experiences you do remember, try to determine how frequently you encountered them during this period. Use these answers to respond to each question:

Never	Rarely	Sometimes	Often	Almost Always
1	2	3	4	5

Since the suicide (or the last GEQ), how often have you:

1. Thought you should go see a doctor?

2. Experienced feeling sick?

3. Experienced trembling, shaking, or twitching?

4. Experienced light-headedness, dizziness, or fainting?

5. Experienced nervousness?

6. Thought that people were uncomfortable offering their condolences to you?

7. Avoided talking about negative or unpleasant things about the deceased?

8. Felt like you just could not make it through another day?

9. Felt like you would never be able to get over the death?

10. Felt anger or resentment towards the deceased after the death?

11. Questioned why the deceased died?

12. Found you couldn't stop thinking about how the death occurred?

13. Thought the decedent's time to die had not yet come?

14. Found yourself not accepting the fact that the death happened?

Never	Rarely	Sometimes	Often	Almost Always
1	2	3	4	5

Since the suicide (or the last GEQ), how often have you:

15. Tried to find a reason to explain the death?

16. Felt avoided by friends?

17. Thought that others didn't want you to talk about the death?

18. Felt like no one cared to listen to you?

19. Felt that neighbors & in-laws did not offer enough concern?

20. Felt like a social outcast?

21. Thought people were gossiping about you or the deceased?

22. Felt like people were probably wondering what kind of personal problems you or the deceased had experienced?

23. Felt like others may have blamed you for the death?

24. Felt like the death somehow reflected negatively on you or your family?

25. Felt somehow stigmatized by the death?

26. Thought of times before the death when you could have made the decedent's life more pleasant?

27. Wished that you hadn't said or done certain things while the deceased was alive?

28. Felt like there was something very important you wanted to make up to the deceased?

29. Felt like maybe you didn't care enough about the deceased?

30. Felt somehow guilty after the death?

31. Felt like the deceased had some kind of complaint against you at the time of the death?

Never	Rarely	Sometimes	Often	Almost Always
1	2	3	4	5

32. Felt that, had you somehow been a different person, the deceased would not have died?

33. Felt like you had made the deceased unhappy long before the death?

34. Felt like you missed an early sign which may have indicated to you that the deceased was not going to be alive much longer?

35. Felt like problems you and the deceased had together contributed to an untimely death?

36. Avoided talking about the death?

37. Felt uncomfortable revealing the cause of the death?

38. Felt embarrassed about the death?

39. Felt uncomfortable about meeting someone who knew you or the deceased?

40. Not mention the death to people you met casually?

41. Felt like the decedent chose to leave you?

42. Felt deserted by the decedent?

43. Felt the death was somehow a deliberate abandonment of you?

44. Felt the deceased never considered what the death might do to you?

45. Sensed some feeling that the deceased rejected you by dying?

46. Felt like you just didn't care enough to take better care of yourself?

47. Found yourself totally preoccupied while driving?

48. Worried that you might harm yourself?

Never	Rarely	Sometimes	Often	Almost Always
1	2	3	4	5

49. Thought of ending your own life?

50. Intentionally tried to hurt yourself?

51. Wondered about the decedent's motivation for not living longer?

52. Felt like the deceased was somehow getting even with you by dying?

53. Felt that you should have somehow prevented the death?

54. Told someone that the cause of death was something different than what it really was?

55. Felt the death was a senseless, wasteful loss of life?

To obtain a detailed assessment of a GEQ, complete the following answer sheet. Please answer all questions. Forward the completed answer sheet, along with a check for $15.00 and a self-addressed envelope, to:

Aftermath Research
University Station Box 5551
Fargo, ND 58105

Confidentiality is assured.

APPENDIX B
GEQ ANSWER SHEET

Name: _____

Mailing Address: _____

_____

_____

You are (circle one): Female   Male

How long has it been since the suicide? _____Yrs & _____Mos

Your age at the time of the suicide: _____ Decedent's age ____

The decedent was your (circle one):
 Son Daughter Husband Wife Father Mother Brother Sister
 Friend Other _____

Circle your answer to each of the 55 GEQ questions:

	Never	Rarely	Sometimes	Often	Almost Always
1.	1	2	3	4	5
2.	1	2	3	4	5
3.	1	2	3	4	5
4.	1	2	3	4	5
5.	1	2	3	4	5
6.	1	2	3	4	5
7.	1	2	3	4	5
8.	1	2	3	4	5
9.	1	2	3	4	5
10.	1	2	3	4	5
11.	1	2	3	4	5
12.	1	2	3	4	5
13.	1	2	3	4	5
14.	1	2	3	4	5
15.	1	2	3	4	5

16. 1	2	3	4	5
17. 1	2	3	4	5
18. 1	2	3	4	5
19. 1	2	3	4	5
20. 1	2	3	4	5
21. 1	2	3	4	5
22. 1	2	3	4	5
23. 1	2	3	4	5
24. 1	2	3	4	5
25. 1	2	3	4	5
26. 1	2	3	4	5
27. 1	2	3	4	5
28. 1	2	3	4	5
29. 1	2	3	4	5
30. 1	2	3	4	5
31. 1	2	3	4	5
32. 1	2	3	4	5
33. 1	2	3	4	5
34. 1	2	3	4	5
35. 1	2	3	4	5
36. 1	2	3	4	5
37. 1	2	3	4	5
38. 1	2	3	4	5
39. 1	2	3	4	5
40. 1	2	3	4	5
41. 1	2	3	4	5
42. 1	2	3	4	5
43. 1	2	3	4	5
44. 1	2	3	4	5
45. 1	2	3	4	5
46. 1	2	3	4	5
47. 1	2	3	4	5
48. 1	2	3	4	5
49. 1	2	3	4	5
50. 1	2	3	4	5
51. 1	2	3	4	5
52. 1	2	3	4	5
53. 1	2	3	4	5
54. 1	2	3	4	5
55. 1	2	3	4	5

REFERENCES

1. Karl A. Menninger. Foreward. In E. Shneidman & N. Farberow (Eds.), *Clues to Suicide*. New York: Mcgraw-Hill Book Co, 1957.

2. R. Hirschfeld & L. Davidson. Risk factors for suicide. In A.J. Frances & R.E. Hales (Eds.), *Review of Psychiatry* (Vol 7). Washington, DC: American Psychiatric Press.

3. Ronald Maris. *Pathways to suicide*. Baltimore: John Hopkins University Press, 1981.

4. M. Kearl & R. Harris. Individualism & the emerging "modern" ideology of death. *Omega, 12*, p. 269-280, 1981.

5. Louis Wekstein. *Handbook of Suicidology: Principles, problems, and practice*. New York: Bruner/Mazel, 1979.

6. G. P. Ginsburg. Public conceptions & attitudes about suicide. *Journal of Health & Social Behavior, 12*, p. 200-207, 1971.

7. Edwin Shneidman. Introduction. In E.Shneidman (Ed.), *Suicidology: Contemporary Developments*. New York: Grune & Stratton, 1976.

8. Alfred Alvarez. *The Savage God: Study of Suicide*. New York: Random House, 1972.

9. Arnold Toynbee. The relationship between life & death, living & dying. In E. Shneidman (Ed.), *Death: Current Perspectives*. Palo Alto: Mayfield, p. 324-332, 1976.

10. Edwin Shneidman. Postvention: The care of the bereaved. *Suicide & Life-Threatening Behavior*, 11, p. 349-359, 1981.

11. Colin Parkes & Robert Weiss. *Recovery from Bereavement*. New York: Basic Books, Inc, 1983.

12. Erich Lindemann. Acute grief: Symptoms & management. *American Journal of Psychiatry*, 101, p. 141-148, 1944.

13. John Bowlby. Process of mourning. *International Journal of Psychoanalysis*, 42, p. 317-340, 1961.

14. Colin Parkes. *Bereavement Studies of Grief in Adult Life*. New York: International University Press, 1972.

15. Edwin Shneidman. Forward. In A. Cain (Ed.), *Survivors of Suicide*. Springfield, Il: C.C. Thomas, 1972.

16. Edwin Shneidman. To the bereaved of a suicide. In B. Danto & A. Kutscher (Eds.), *Suicide & Bereavement*. New York: Arno Press, p. 67-69, 1977.

17. Wayne Weiten. *Psychology: Themes and variations*. Pacific Grove, CA: Brooks/Cole, p. 547, 1989.

18. John Hewett. *After Suicide*. Philadelphia: Westminster Press, 1980.

19. Samuel Wallace. The cost of suicide. In S. Wallace (Ed.), *After Suicide*. New York: John Wiley & Sons, p. 229-244, 1973.

20. Erich Lindemann & Ina Greer. A study of grief emotional responses to suicide. *Pastoral Psychology*, 4, p. 9-13, 1953.

21. Colin Parkes. The broken heart. In E. Shneidman (Ed.), *Death: Current Perspectives*. Palo Alto: Mayfield, p. 333-346, 1976.

22. Kjell Erik Rudestam. Physical & psychological responses to suicide in the family. *Journal of Consulting & Clinical Psychology*, 45, p. 162-170, 1977.

23. Karl A. Menninger. *Man against himself*. New York: Halcourt Brace Jovanovich, 1938.

24. William Steele. *Preventing teenage suicide: The second leading cause of death among the nation's youth*. Naples, FL: Ann Arbor Publishers, 1983.

25. Edwin Shneidman. Prevention, intervention, & postvention. *Annals of Internal Medicine*, 75, p. 453-458, 1971.

26. M. Goldberg & E. Mudd. The effects of suicidal behavior upon marriage and the family. In L. P. Resnik (Ed.), *Suicidal Behavior: Diagnosis and Management*. Boston: Little, Brown, p. 348-356, 1968.

27. Edward Dunne & Karen Dunne-Maxim. Preface. In E. Dunne, J. McIntosh, & K. Dunne-Maxim (Eds.), *Suicide and its aftermath: Understanding and counseling the survivors*. New York: W.W. Norton & Company, 1987.

28. Mark Solomon. The bereaved & stigma of suicide. *Omega, 13*, p. 377-387, 1982.

29. Charles Neuringer. Bereavement reactions in survivors of suicide. In B. Danto & A. Kutscher (Eds.), *Suicide & Bereavement*. New York: Arno Press, p. 150-162, 1977.

30. Robert Kastenbaum. Suicide as a preferred way of death. In E.Shneidman (Ed.), *Suicidology: Contemporary Developments*. New York: Grune & Stratton, p. 421-441, 1976.

31. Pamela Cantor. The effects of youthful suicide on the family. *Psychiatric Opinion*, 12, p. 6-11, 1975.

32. Victor E. Frankl. *Man's Search for Meaning*. Boston: Beacon Press, 1959.

33. John McIntosh. Survivor family relationships: Literature review. In E. Dunne, J. McIntosh, & K. Dunne-Maxim (Eds.), *Suicide and its aftermath: Understanding and counseling the survivors*. New York: W.W. Norton & Company, 1987.

34. William Coleman. *Understanding Suicide*. Elgin, IL.: David C. Cook Publishing Co, 1979.

35. Edwin Shneidman. *Deaths of Man*. New York: Quadrangle Books, 1973.

36. Lee Ann Hoff. Helping survivors of suicide. In *People in Crisis: Understanding & Helping*, p. 142-147, 1978.

37. Donna Junghardt. A program in postvention. In C. Hatton, S. Valente, & A. Rink (Eds.), *Suicide: Assessment & Intervention*. New York: Appleton, Century, Crofts, p. 124-132, 1977.

38. Allen Battle. Group therapy for survivors of suicide. *Crisis, 5*, p. 45-58, 1984.

39. Adina Wrobleski. The suicide survivors grief group. *Omega, 15*, p. 173-184, 1984.

40. Bruce Danto. Project SOS: Volunteers in action with survivors of suicide. In B. Danto & A. Kutscher (Eds.), *Suicide & Bereavement*. New York: Arno Press, p. 222-239, 1977.

41. Terence Barrett & Thomas Scott. The Grief Experience Questionnaire. *Suicide & Life-Threatening Behavior*, 19(2), p. 201-215, 1989.